THE
WONDERS OF MASSABIELLE
AT
LOURDES

Our Lady of Lourdes

THE WONDERS OF MASSABIELLE AT LOURDES

Apparitions · Miracles · Pilgrimages

A NARRATIVE IN
THIRTY-TWO PARTS ADAPTED TO
MAY OR OCTOBER DEVOTIONS

BY

THE REV. S. PRUVOST

Translated from the French by
REV. JOSEPH A. FREDETTE

Foreword by
THE RT. REV. JOSEPH H. McMAHON

With thirty-one illustrations

Published by
THE LOURDES COMPANY
270 CONGRESS STREET
BOSTON, MASS.

Nihil Obstat

P. E. DESJARDINS
J. A. CAREY
Censores Librorum

Imprimatur

✠ JOHN GREGORY MURRAY, D. D.
Bishop of Portland, Me.

October 12, 1925

Respectfully Dedicated to

His Lordship John Gregory Murray, D.D.

on the occasion of his accession to the

See of Portland, Me.

DECLARATION OF THE AUTHOR

In conformity with the decree of Pope Urban VIII (1625), I hereby declare that if in the course of this work I have qualified as miracles certain marvelous incidents which have not as yet been submitted to a canonical examination, I have had no other intention in mind than to present them as certified by private testimony and not as having been approved by our Holy Church, to which alone belongs the right to decide authoritatively in such matters.

S. P.

AUTHOR'S PREFACE

THESE pages have been written on the strength of the veracity of the chief historians of Our Lady of Lourdes, —First, Mr. Estrade and Dr. Dozous who witnessed the marvels they so accurately describe, and,—Second, Mr. Lasserre, whose lengthy and judicious investigations give to this narrative a guarantee of loyalty and genuineness which defy the most subtle criticism. To the detailed account of the eighteen apparitions and of the first miracles which so wonderfully corroborated them almost from the start, not only at Lourdes but throughout the world, we have added the story of the establishment and progress of the celebrated pilgrimage with sufficient details to satisfy the pious curiosity of the majority of the faithful. Those who would require additional data relative to these historic facts may consult the authors just mentioned. As for the criticism of the miracle, both scientific and philosophical, they may read with advantage the learned treatises of Dr. Boissarie, chief of the Medical Clinic at Lourdes, and a work by Canon G. Bertrin, the eminent professor at the Catholic Faculties of Paris, which contains the most practical treatise ever written on miracles.

But this modest work of ours appeals to a different public. Though its aim is less pretentious, it is animated with the same spirit: a devotion full of confidence and love to the Immaculate Mary, and genuine gratitude for the innumerable favors she has bestowed upon the world ever since she deigned to visit us in person.

Glory and love to Jesus and Mary!

We deposit this little book at Their feet in grateful homage.

The Bishop's House
307 Congress Street
Portland, Maine

January 24, 1926

My Dear Father Fredette:

Your beautiful little work, "The Wonders of Massabielle at Lourdes," gave me more pleasure than any book that I have read in many a day. The method of treating the incidents in the life and experience of Blessed Bernadette is so frank and logical, the narrative is so simple and straightforward, the language is so direct and trenchant, the scenes are depicted with such power, free from all attempt at ornament or special pleading, that I would pity the person who could read the book and not be touched to the depths of his soul. Here, indeed, is the indisputable evidence that the supernatural power of performing miracles entrusted to the Apostles by our Divine Master is still exercised by the Spirit of God in our day to open the eyes of the blind, to give hearing to the deaf and to elevate those who already live the spiritual life of the children of God to more enchanting heights of union with the Spouse of Christ.

The little spiritual bouquet at the conclusion of each chapter makes the book most serviceable for public reading in the churches as well as for the sodality meetings.

With best wishes for a wide circulation of this apostle of faith, I remain,

Yours faithfully in Xto,

John J. Murray

FOREWORD

IT is with great pleasure that I contribute these few words of approval to this latest contribution in English to the scores of books that are spreading throughout the world the knowledge of that marvelous shrine of the Blessed Mother of God in the Pyrenees known as the Home of the Miracle.

The recent beatification of Bernadette Soubirous has once more focused attention upon the favored child of Lourdes whose humility in seeking and maintaining seclusion in her convent home at Nevers far from the Grotto where she had been the recipient of such signal marks of predilection has now been rewarded by her elevation to the honors of the altar. *Exaltavit humiles:* He hath exalted them of low degree.

In the chapters of this book will be found, told in simple language, the fascinating story of the apparitions of the Virgin to the child and the wonderful results accruing therefrom, results which have had their repercussion throughout the world. *Visitasti terram et inebriasti eam: multiplicasti locupletare eam.*

I am informed that even in manuscript this book has served to edify throngs of worshippers at devotions during May and October. Knowing how difficult it is for priests to find interesting matter to use on such occasions I am sure they will welcome this little volume whose practical value has been successfully tested.

I fondly hope that it will help greatly to spread widely the knowledge of our gracious Lady of Lourdes, so that her clientele may be numerously increased among those who are sick in soul, wearied and perhaps maimed in body, who will be comforted by the thought of her loving interest in all that concerns them, temporally and spiritually.

JOSEPH H. McMAHON,

Pastor of the Church of Our Lady of Lourdes

NEW YORK

Feast of St. Michel, 1925.

CONTENTS

A. M. D. G.

ILLUSTRATIONS

THE
WONDERS OF MASSABIELLE
AT
LOURDES

CHAPTER I
LOURDES AND THE GAVE
The Soubirous Family—Bernadette at Bartrès

WHAT marvelous events have taken place at Lourdes since the Blessed Virgin deigned to appear there and converse as many as eighteen times with a little shepherdess, a poor ignorant child of fourteen!

Once again does the world realize that God makes use of the most humble means to obtain great results. Isn't the Blessed Virgin herself a most striking example of this divine method? Who could have imagined that the testimony of this little child would have reëchoed throughout the world, attracting to this particular spot in the Pyrenees ever-increasing throngs, transforming this little ancient village into a modern up-to-date city, displacing the stony bed of a large and impetuous river, and covering with superb basilicas the once barren and savage cliffs on the mountain side! And yet, all these marvels are to-day a reality which no one would dare question. The true Christian views them with joy and gratitude, for they are the reward of his piety and of his faith; the unbeliever stands baffled and astounded, and if he be an avowed enemy of the supernatural he becomes all the more infuriated as he finds himself unable to discredit them. Under one form or another, regardless of the sentiment that produces it, the belief in the marvels of Lourdes is as universal as the reputation of this hitherto deserted and obscure hamlet.

Many Christians have been blessed with the unique privilege of kneeling before the Grotto, immortalized by the memorable visit of the Virgin Mary, and this cherished memory accompanies them through life. And how many others there are, a little less fortunate, who live in hopes of visiting Lourdes some day! Pilgrims of desire, let them fly in thought and love to Mary's beloved Grotto and pay homage to her, for this is the spot which she sanctified by the tread of her virginal feet and to which all nations are invited.

In our daily considerations we will set forth the story of the apparitions of the Heavenly Queen, the first miracles, the beginning and the development of the now celebrated pilgrimage. From these narratives we will derive an ever-increasing love for Mary, a more solid faith in the truths she came to confirm, a stronger hope in the divine promises, and a more profound devotion to the Blessed Eucharist; for, at Lourdes as elsewhere, Mary appeared to the world that her Divine Son might be better known and better loved. *"Ad Jesum per Mariam,* (To Jesus through Mary),"* to quote the devout St. Bernard.

To-day we will acquaint ourselves with Lourdes, the privileged home of all these marvels, and also with the fortunate child who became their foremost witness and intermediary.

The city of Lourdes, the chief seat of a canton in

the department of the Upper Pyrenees, is located at
the base of the first spur of the mountain chain which
separates France from Spain.

At the time of the apparitions it numbered about
four thousand inhabitants; to-day, especially during the
pilgrimage season, this figure is increased to fifty thous-
and. Its history, particularly in the old days, has been
most varied. At the time of the great Asiatic invasions
it was often visited and subsequently destroyed by the
barbarians. Some years afterwards, although protected
by a seemingly impregnable fortress erected in its very
midst, it was taken by the Saracens only to be retaken
by Charlemagne. In turn the English took possession
of the city during the "Hundred Year War." It is
situated on the right bank of the Gave, the most important river of the province. Issuing from the glaciers
of Gavarnie near Spain the Gave rolls its noisy waters
down the mountain sides, at times in fantastic leaps and
most picturesque cascades, until it reaches the plains of
Lourdes. Here it continues in a westerly direction,
passing the city of Pau and uniting its waters with those
of the Adour, whence it speeds on to the Atlantic near
Bayonne. It is on the banks of this stream that all the
events which we are about to narrate have taken place.

There lived at Lourdes a good pious family which
had been reduced in recent years to the most abject
poverty. The father, François Soubirous, and the
mother Louise Castérot, both honest people and staunch
Christians, were at the time of their marriage in fair

circumstances. They rented the Boly mill which is situated on the Lapaca stream at the foot of the fortress. It is here that Mrs. Soubirous, on January 7, 1844, gave birth to her first child whom they christened *Bernadette*, the future heroine of the marvelous history of Lourdes. At the age of five months the infant was confided to the care of a remarkable peasant family named Aravant-Lagües in the village of Bartrès, about two miles from Lourdes. There she remained until the age of three when she was taken back home. Some years later she returned to Bartrès where she was given the care of her foster parents' sheep during the harvesting season. On this occasion she remained one full year.

At the Soubirous home a surprising change had come over the family; poverty stared them in the face. In proportion as the family increased, business at the mill declined,—to such an extent that in 1855 Mr. Sourbirous was compelled to abandon his mill and content himself with the life and income of an ordinary laborer. His good wife, despite her feeble constitution, struggled to give her six children the necessary attention, so that after all, Bernadette's absence from home where bread was often lacking was in reality a veritable relief.

In this arrangement of events can we not discern a secret plan of Divine Providence Who, in order to attain His object, has frequently chosen His messengers among shepherdesses? Thus we have St. Genevieve of Nanterre who saved Paris; St. Solange, the illustrious patron saint of Berry; the immortal Joan of Arc;

BERNADETTE SOUBIROUS
At the time of the apparitions

St. Germaine, the thaumaturgus of Pibrac; and many others. Bernadette was still occupied as a shepherdess when she attained the age of fourteen, spending her time on the solitary hillside in company with her sheep. She was weak in appearance and quite short in stature for her age; her health was poor and she frequently gave way to oppressions caused by asthma; her intellect was most common, her memory deficient. As she had never attended school, she was therefore unable to read and spoke only in the Pyrenean dialect. As for her knowledge, it could be summed up in those prayers which compose the rosary, her favorite devotion: "Our Father,—Hail Mary!—I Believe in God,—Glory be to the Father." . . . Instinctively pious she recited these prayers over and over, keeping at the same time a vigilant watch over her flock. Her natural infirmities as well as her weak, untrained mind were in a measure compensated by some very remarkable traits. Her features, perfectly outlined, were at the same time sympathetic and attractive; an amiable smile reflecting the peace and purity of her soul illumined them constantly. She had not as yet made her first communion so her parents, notwithstanding their extreme poverty, decided to recall her that she might attend the parochial catechism classes as well as those of the Sisters' school and thus prepare herself for this great event of a Christian's life. It was in the latter part of January, 1858, therefore, that Bernadette bade farewell to her foster parents who had learned to love her as their own child and returned to Lourdes. We presently find the

Soubirous occupying one of the most miserable dwellings of the city on a street called Petits Fossés. (This same house to-day carries the number 15.) Here again do we not perceive the designs of Divine Providence Who, at this remarkable moment, brings our little shepherdess back to her native home to receive from the lips of our Heavenly Queen a glorious, a most merciful mission!

How different from our own are the ways of God! The world abhors the idea of poverty; it despises the poor and God honors them. If He wishes to confide a message to an earthly being, does He choose from the ranks of the rich? No, but rather from the lowly and the poor. Such was the case at the time of the Incarnation; it is an obscure virgin of Nazareth who becomes the glorious Mother of the Son of God made man.

Let us learn from all this never to envy perishable riches if we are poor, and to keep our hearts aloof from them if they have been thrust upon us.

INVOCATION

Hail, Mary.

"O Holy Virgin Mary, seat of wisdom, thou who hast so magnificently proclaimed in thy hymn of thanksgiving for the wonders of the Incarnation the glories of humility and poverty, grant us the grace of dealing with all earthly possessions in such a way that we may never lose sight of the wondrous gifts which God has in store for us in the blessed eternity.

"Our Lady of Lourdes, pray for us." (Three hundred days of indulgence. Decree of November 9, 1907.)

CHAPTER II

FIRST APPARITION

The Grotto of Massabielle—The Savy Mill

BERNADETTE had been home for about a fortnight when on the eleventh day of February, Mrs. Soubirous finding that her store of wood had all but disappeared, despatched Mary, her second daughter, to gather a fresh supply along the banks of the Gave. Bernadette begged to accompany her sister. The good mother hesitated, fearing that the cool atmosphere might be injurious to the child's weak constitution. However, after listening to the entreaties of a young neighbor, Jeanne Abadie, a friend of the two sisters, she consented, cautioning Bernadette to wear her stockings and to cover her head and shoulders with her "capulet," a style of hood most common among the women of that region. Permission thus granted, the three little girls strolled joyously along in quest of dry wood. They headed straight for a spot called Massabielle, a rugged cliff rising perpendicularly from the left bank of the Gave. At the foot of this cliff nature had chiselled in the rock a deep cavity in the shape of an irregular dome measuring from fourteen to sixteen feet in height, from twenty to twenty-five in length, and twenty-two at its greatest depth. In the upper right hand corner, a passage which resembled a reclining chimney found its way through the rock to a Gothic-like opening where the light penetrated. Ordinarily this Grotto was quite inaccessible. To reach it one would leave the town after crossing the Old Bridge, follow a steep path called The Road to the Forest, and when near the spot where the upper basilica was since erected, descend the precipitous cliff of Massabielle until he reached the banks of the river just beyond the Grotto. Direct approach from the city was cut off by a canal called Le Savy, which, after emerging from the Gave just below the Old Bridge, rejoined the stream at this particular spot. The stretch of land situated between the canal and the Gave constituted, thereby, an island commonly known as the Savy Prairie. Le Savy furnished power to an old mill which had been idle for repairs; and precisely for this reason its waters were very low.

Taking advantage of this fortunate occurrence the young girls chose the direction of the mill as the easiest means of reaching the Gave. Once opposite the Grotto, Jeanne and Mary, their shoes in hand, waded across the canal; but as Bernadette was compelled to remove her stockings, she lingered behind fearing most naturally the low temperature of the water. Eventually, she decided to follow and had already begun to lower her stockings when suddenly her attention was arrested by a most mysterious occurrence. But pray, let her relate the following happenings herself, and let us copy her narrative precisely as it came from the lips of Mr.

Estrade, the man who wrote about the apparitions and who translated literally Bernadette's Pyrenean dialect.

"I had started to remove one stocking when suddenly I was startled by a peculiar noise which resembled the roar of an approaching storm. I glanced about me, at the trees which lined the river bank, but all was still; I must have been mistaken. I resumed the task of removing my stockings when lo! the same mysterious sound reached my ears. This time I became frightened and I stood erect; I remained there speechless not knowing what to think, when presently, as I turned and looked in the direction of the Grotto I noticed in one of the openings of the cliff a bush being stirred as if by a strong wind. At the same time I beheld within the Grotto a glittering cloud of gold; and almost simultaneously there appeared before my dazzled eyes at the edge of the opening just over the bush, a lady both young and beautiful, beautiful beyond description. She gazed tenderly at me, smiled, and bade me to come nearer, as if she had been my mother. The sense of fear had vanished but I could not figure out where I was. I rubbed my eyes, I closed and opened them alternately but the lady was always there, smiling gently and assuring me that I was not mistaken. Without realizing what I was doing, I took my beads from my pocket and knelt down. By a movement of her head the lady clearly indicated that my action was pleasing to her and her fingers reached for a rosary which she herself carried on her right arm. As I was about to begin the recitation of the prayers I endeavored to make the sign of the cross but my arm remained as if paralyzed and it was only after the lady had made it herself that I was able to follow her example. She was content to let me pray alone; her fingers slipped from bead to bead as I recited the succession of 'Hail Marys' but her lips remained motionless; it was only at the end of each decade that she repeated with me: 'Glory be to the Father, to the Son and to the Holy Ghost.' At the completion of the rosary the lady disappeared, together with the gilded cloud which had enshrouded her."

Such was Bernadette's narrative. She did not know who the lady might be; yet, the latter's attitude during the recitation of the beads might have enlightened her had she possessed some education. Of all the prayers that compose the rosary, Mary could recite but one only,—the "Gloria," which is a praise to the Almighty. The "Credo," the symbol of our faith is an earthly virtue which consists in believing what we do not see; in Heaven, where the elect come face to face with God, it is no longer a matter of faith but pure evidence. The "Pater" is a prayer addressed to the Heavenly Father by man who is still an exile on earth; and Mary, who is no longer of this world, has nothing to ask since she enjoys the plenitude of happiness. As for the "Ave Maria," it is a prayer of praise and supplication offered up to our Heavenly Queen; she cannot therefore recite it herself. By using her rosary, Mary encourages us to recite it, clearly showing how attentive she is to our prayers and how she counts every "Ave Maria," showering in turn as many maternal blessings.

Bernadette's companions, Jeanne and Mary, actively engaged in their search for wood, had not given the girl a thought. But presently they turned, saw her kneeling, and jesting, they called her. The child instantly arose and descended into the water which she found to her great astonishment and according to her own words "as warm as dish water." After the girls had collected a sufficient quantity of dry wood they ascended the steep Massabielle cliff to regain the road that led to the city. As they trudged along Bernadette remarked:

"Did you not see anything strange at the Grotto?"

"No," replied the girls, "why do you ask?"

"Oh! nothing," continued the child, feigning indifference.

Jeanne, due to her more rapid strides, had soon outdistanced her companions. Left alone with her sister, Mary insisted upon knowing the import of Bernadette's remarks; and it was only after she had promised absolute secrecy, that the child described the remarkable vision. But Mary's promise was not to be kept for as soon as they reached home she lost no time in imparting the news to her mother. "That is most childish," remarked Mrs. Soubirous, as she gazed at Bernadette; "you were mistaken, my child, you simply allowed your imagination to get the best of you; at all events I forbid you to return to the Grotto!" This order struck deep in the child's heart for she had but one desire— that of seeing the lady once more. Her soul was filled with the sweet memory of the vision, the details of which were constantly before her mind. Evening came, and after eating a frugal supper all knelt in reverence for the recitation in common of the evening prayer. It was Bernadette who recited the prayer aloud. According to her custom she always ended by the thrice repeated invocation: "O Mary, conceived without sin, pray for us who have recourse to thee." After the first invocation a sob muffled her voice; she continued but the words were choked in her throat. "What is the trouble?" asked the disturbed mother. And as she stared at her daughter she beheld two tears drop from her eyes. "Mother," said the child, "I feel the necessity of weeping." There was no sleep for Bernadette that night; "the august features of the lady," as she afterwards related, "were ever before me, and I could not convince myself that I had been mistaken." The following days, Friday and Saturday, were days of sorrowful anxiety. Bernadette who had never disobeyed, shuddered at the thought that she was never to return to Massabielle where she had received a foretaste of Heaven. Her mother endeavored to argue with her but the child remained firm in her conviction; she had seen and heard quite distinctly the wonderful lady recite in company with her at the close of each decade, the prayer "Glory be to the Father." No, there could be no doubt, it must have been an angel or a saint from Heaven.   The angel of darkness, whom her mother had often mentioned to frighten her, could not have made the sign of the cross nor recite the praise to the august Trinity.   Bernadette was ignorant but her common sense could not admit of such an error. Time will prove how well she reasoned.

INVOCATION

Hail, Mary.

"O Mother of our Saviour, thy first lesson to Bernadette was the devotion to the sorrowful passion of thy Divine Son, in teaching her to make with fervor and respect the sign of the cross. Impress upon our souls the great necessity of this devotion, that we may understand more and more that, in the cross alone, lies our salvation.

"Our Lady of Lourdes, pray for us."

CHAPTER III
SECOND APPARITION
The Holy Water

SUNDAY came; an interior voice both sweet and powerful spoke thus to Bernadette: "Return to Massabielle." Alas! the order to keep away from the Grotto was a formal one and the dear child had never disobeyed. As she was loath to bring the subject up again to her mother, she begged her sister to intervene. But the good mother would listen to no argument. Jeanne Abadie was next to intercede in her little friend's behalf but all in vain. After dinner Mrs. Soubirous speaking rather sharply: "Well, go along; but be sure and return for Vespers; if you fail, remember what I have in store for you." The good mother hoped that this second visit to the Grotto, where Bernadette would see nothing out of the ordinary, would surely cure her daughter of her illusions. Thereupon, the two sisters left the house. A dozen or more young girls to whom Mary had confided the entire story soon joined them. One of the companions suggested, as a matter of precaution, that a bottle of holy water be taken along with which to sprinkle the apparition as is generally the custom in manifestations of the evil spirit. When all was in readiness the young girls split up in two groups, —Bernadette, radiant with joy and hope heading the first group. Arriving at the Grotto, she knelt opposite the bush where the lady had appeared to her and without delay she began the recitation of the rosary. Suddenly overcome with ecstasy and delight she cried out: "There she is, there she is!" Instantly one of the girls handed Bernadette the bottle of holy water, saying: "Throw holy water upon her!" The visionary having sprinkled the apparition turned to her companions, saying: "She doesn't appear offended; on the contrary, she seems perfectly satisfied and she smiles to us all." The entire company profoundly impressed kneels in reverence, for one look at Bernadette suffices to convince them that something extraordinary is taking place. She is motionless; her features, marvelously transfigured, radiate with a light beyond all human conception. Her companions, dumbfounded and speechless with emotion, realize that they are witnessing a supernatural phenomenon even though they do not grasp its character. Their emotion is such that they soon become terror-stricken and sobs are heard on all sides. "If Bernadette should die!" cried one of the group. And the child, always motionless with eyes fixed upon the vision, appeared absolutely oblivious of all that surrounded her. Presently two women attracted by the cries of the girl hasten from the neighboring mill; these are the mother and sister of Nicolau, the miller.

At the sight of Bernadette in ecstasy, they approach her with reverence; they speak to her and endeavor to bring her back to herself. But all in vain! The child sees nothing, hears nothing, all her senses and faculties are concentrated upon the vision. Thereupon, Mrs. Nicolau returned to the mill and bade her son to come in all haste. The miller, a young man of twenty-eight, obeyed the summons. As he approached the scene, it was noticed that a smile covered his features for he was reluctant to believe all that his mother had told him. And yet at the sight of Bernadette, his scepticism vanished; a deep sense of veneration came over him, for he realized that the scene which was taking place before his eyes bordered on the supernatural. For a long time he observed the child, not daring to approach her, and it was only after repeated entreaties on the part of the mother that he took her by the arm, raised her, and endeavored to have her walk. But Bernadette remained perfectly insensible; her eyes fixed upon the divine object, and an ecstatic smile still illumining her countenance, she allowed herself to be taken away, almost carried bodily towards the mill by the miller and his mother. There only did she emerge from her ecstasy. But at the same time the heavenly joy that transformed her features disappeared and gave way to a touch of sadness. For the poor child, it was the realization of finding herself once more upon earth after having enjoyed a glimpse of Heaven. All those present questioned her most minutely relative to the vision, and this is her description of the lady as she appeared to her for the second time:

"She has the appearance of a young girl of sixteen; clothed in white, a blue ribbon girdles her waist, and falls loosely at her side; a white veil covering her head and all but concealing her hair droops gracefully on her back; her feet are bare, although covered by the lower folds of her garment, with the exception of the extremities which are adorned with brilliant yellow roses; she carries on her right arm a rosary of white beads linked together by a chain of gold as resplendent as the roses which grace her feet."

By this time Bernadette's companions had reached the city and had related all that they had seen. Her sister Mary, as she opened the door of her home, was so overcome that her sobs prevented her from speaking. Mrs. Soubirous, baffled for a moment and fearing that something serious had befallen her daughter, dashed out of the house and hastened to the Grotto. Luckily, a few women met her on the way who reassured her; and yet, if her fears were allayed, her displeasure increased in proportion. She made straight for the Savy mill, whip in hand, with the idea of chastising her daughter. "What do you mean, you little clown? Do you wish to make of us all the laughing stock of our community? I'll put a quick end to these so-called visions and tales of a lady!" And as she raised her arm menacingly, the miller's wife intervened, saying: "What are you doing? What has your daughter done that you should treat her thus? Bernadette is an angel of Heaven, do you understand? I shall never forget her attitude at the Grotto." Having suddenly regained her composure, the mother, broken with emotion, sat and wept bitterly as she gazed at her child. After a few moments, having recovered sufficiently she seized her daughter by the hand and the two returned to the city.

The happy visionary was as yet quite ignorant of the heavenly lady's identity. In her ecstasies she was no longer herself; instead of speaking to her she always knelt in profound contemplation. The effect of this second meeting was to dispel the child's timidity, and to establish between herself and the supernatural being a sort of familiarity filled with confidence and love.

INVOCATION

Hail, Mary.

"O Mary, Queen of the angels and of the saints, thou whose glory and beauty adorn the Heavens, grant us the grace of living and dying in such purity of body and soul that some day we may have the happiness of contemplating thee in the eternal vision of Heaven.

"Our Lady of Lourdes, pray for us."

CHAPTER IV

THIRD APPARITION

Madame Millet and Mademoiselle Peyret
Request and Promise

THE tales of the Grotto were the talk of the town. Certain people though inclined to discredit them, were nevertheless astounded over the apparent sincerity of the young girls who unwound their narratives without ever contradicting themselves. But as a rule, they were ridiculed and treated as silly schemes. All these rumors brought to the Soubirous home an influx of visitors eager to obtain some information. One Wednesday evening, two ladies, Madame Millet and Mademoiselle Antoinette Peyret, called at the house. As they entered, Mrs. Soubirous was in the act of scolding Bernadette very severely because of the child's reiterated plea to be allowed to return to the Grotto. She would not hear of it, alleging as a pretext the child's delicate constitution. The two visitors courteously advised the mother that it might be well to accede to the child's legitimate desire lest her health suffer as a consequence of her efforts being forever frustrated. "Would you then make of my child," remarked Mrs. Soubirous, "an object of ridicule?" "Far be it from us, Madame; but pray let us tell you before taking leave that you are assuming a tremendous responsibility; who knows if you are not thwarting the designs of God?" This was a direct challenge to the staunch faith which always characterized Mrs. Soubirous; it was more than she could bear. Overflowing with emotion, she grasped their hands saying: "My mind is wandering. . . . It doesn't appear that you are deceiving me. . . . I confide my child to your care. . . . Consider the agony of my soul. . . . Watch over her." . . . It was subsequently arranged that the following morning Mme. Millet and Mlle. Peyret would accompany Bernadette to the Grotto. Before dawn they reached the Soubirous home where they found Bernadette waiting for them. Together they went to church and attended Mass, thereby placing their mission in the hands of Divine Providence; they then proceeded to Massabielle. Dawn was approaching slowly; but the stillness of the night was as yet undisturbed. Secretly, Mme. Millet had brought a blessed candle and Mlle. Peyret, paper, pen, and ink.

How Bernadette longed to arrive at her cherished Grotto! Unfortunately, access by way of the mill was no longer possible. The repairs having been completed, the water-gates had been reopened and the canal flooded, so that the only alternative was the difficult path through the forest. Preceding her companions, the young girl, inwardly attracted, fairly leaped as she scaled the rocks of Massabielle and descended to the Grotto. When the two ladies arrived

FRANCOIS SOUBIROUS
Bernadette's father

LOUISE CASTEROT
Mrs. Soubirous, Bernadette's mother

JEAN-MARIE SOUBIROUS
A brother of Bernadette

MARIE SOUBIROUS
One of Bernadette's sisters

they found the child already kneeling in front of the niche and reciting her rosary. They immediately lighted their candle and knelt beside her. After a short interval Bernadette uttered a cry of exultation: "She is coming! She is here!" And she prostrated herself to the ground, hysterical with joy. Her two companions saw nothing but the wild rosebush and the cold bleak rocks; still, one glance at the visionary was enough to convince them that the mysterious lady was truly there. She prayed and smiled alternately; and yet she was not in ecstasy, for she maintained her self-possession and communicated with those around her. The recitation of the rosary ended, Mlle. Peyret, handing Bernadette the pen and paper she had brought with her, said: "Ask the lady if she has any communication to make and let her give it to us in writing." Bernadette seized the objects and advanced towards the bush. Noticing that her companions followed her she bade them remain behind. Rising on tip-toe, with outstretched hands she presented the pen and paper to the lady. In this posture she remained for some little time apparently listening to a voice from the niche. Finally lowering her hands, she made a deep prostration and returned to her place.

"What was the lady's answer?" asked Mlle. Peyret.

"She smiled," replied Bernadette, "saying: 'What I have to communicate to you, I need not do in writing.' Then after a short pause she added: 'Will you be kind enough to come here for a fortnight?'"

"And what did you answer?"

"I answered 'yes.'"

"But why does the lady wish you to come here?"

"I do not know; she did not tell me."

"And why," asked Mme. Millet, "did you beckon us to remain in the rear as we proceeded towards the niche with you?"

"In obedience to the lady."

"Ask her then if my presence here is displeasing to her."

Bernadette lifted her eyes in the direction of the Grotto, then turned about saying: "The lady answers: 'No, her presence here is not unwelcome.'"

After a few moments Bernadette called Mlle. Peyret's attention, saying: "Antoinette, the lady is gazing at you now."

"Ask her," exclaimed the young lady with emotion, "if she would object to our accompanying you here during the fortnight." To this question voiced by Bernadette the lady replied:

"They may come with you, and many others also; I wish to see many people here."

This entire scene lasted approximately one hour; then the vision disappeared. Immediately Bernadette rose to her feet and prepared to return. As they strolled homeward her companions questioned her uninterruptedly.

"You conversed quite lengthily with this lady; what more did she tell you?"

"She told me: 'I promise to make you happy, not in this world, but in the next.'"

"Did you ask her name?"

"Yes;—she lowered her head and smiled but did not answer."

Arriving at the Soubirous home, the two women related their impressions to the mother and remarked as they left: "Oh! how fortunate you are to be the mother of such a child!"

The portrayal of this third apparition suggests many important reflections: First—The Celestial Lady gazed benevolently upon Mme. Millet, but more so upon Mlle. Peyret. Can we not suppose that the Blessed Virgin, by concentrating her maternal attention upon the latter, wished by so doing to favor and reward the girl who, as a member of the Congregation of the Children of Mary, was especially consecrated to her? Second—She had said to Bernadette: "Will you kindly come here for a fortnight?" And who speaks thus? It is the Queen of Heaven, who has the right to command the universe; it is the Mother of God, the most exalted of all creatures. And to whom does she speak? To a poor ignorant, insignificant child according to the judgment of the world,—to the most despicable thing in existence; she does not command, she begs. What condescension, and what a lesson for us all! How she makes us understand that our real worth lies in the soul and is measured by our innocence and humility! These qualities in Bernadette's heart meant more to our

Blessed Lady than all the earthly gifts which we prize so highly: fortune, beauty, nobility, science. It is this very thought that Mary expressed in her "Magnificat": "He was pleased with the humility of His servant. He exalted the humble." Third—And again she said: "I promise to make you happy, not in this world, but in the next." Thus did Christ speak to His Apostles on the eve of His death. He told them to expect tribulations of all kinds during this mortal life, but at the same time He promised them happiness beyond the grave. We are created for happiness, but it is not here that we should seek it. This life is but a series of trials and miseries; by accepting them with patience and resignation, by avoiding sin and practicing virtue, they are soon transformed into a path of roses which leads to Heaven, the one and only abode of happiness. What a lesson of wisdom! Alas! how many are there who reject it!

INVOCATION

Hail, Mary.

"O Mary, thou who didst attain the height of glory thou possessest, only through intense agony whilst on earth, grant us the grace of perfectly understanding the price of sufferings, and of appreciating the vast merits derived therefrom, that, after this mortal life, we may have the happiness of exchanging them for the eternal joys of Paradise.

"Our Lady of Lourdes, pray for us."

CHAPTER V

FOURTH AND FIFTH APPARITIONS

Mother Soubirous and Aunt Bernarde
Infernal Noises—Prayer

BERNADETTE had promised the lady to visit the Grotto every day for a fortnight. When she imparted this bit of news to her parents they became very much disturbed for the publicity surrounding them had caused these poor people no little uneasiness. And all this time, who could the mysterious lady be? Did she come from Heaven or hell? The people of that region recalled having heard of diabolical scenes enacted years ago at Massabielle; hence the fear that this spot held for the natives. Might it not be a repetition of these dreadful disorders? In their perplexity they resolved to seek the advice of Aunt Bernarde, Mrs. Soubirous's sister, as well as Bernadette's godmother whom they had frequently consulted in difficult matters. After mature reflection, Aunt Bernarde advised them to cease all opposition and to accompany their child to the Grotto, in order to become better acquainted with the whole situation. "How much better," said she, "had this been done at the outset!"

It was therefore decided that on the following day, Friday, mother Soubirous and Bernadette were to proceed to the Grotto, stopping on their way to take Aunt

Bernarde. And it took place as planned. When they arrived, already one hundred persons were there waiting. Without hesitation Bernadette went and knelt at her customary spot, and taking her rosary she made a sign of the cross which impressed all the bystanders. The lady was already there and the ecstasy began. A most resplendent light illumined the child's features and her eyes sparkled, ardent and soft as two stars; her body was inclined forward as though prepared for a flight heavenward. Both the mother and the aunt gazed at her with mixed admiration and fear. "My God!" cried the mother, " do not take away my child!" "How beautiful she is!" cried another voice. All eyes were filled with tears at the sight of such an extraordinary spectacle. After a half hour the child emerged from her ecstasy and resumed her natural self; she rubbed her eyes and appeared overwhelmed by the extent of her happiness. With a loving smile on her countenance she arose and turned towards her mother and her aunt. How tenderly, how respectfully the two women embraced her! Together they returned to their home. On the way, Bernadette related a very strange incident that occurred during the ecstasy but which was hidden from the people. Most terrifying voices appeared to rise from the bosom of the earth in the direction of the Gave; they could be heard to defy, contradict and strike one another in imitation of the shrieks and yells of an infuriated mob. One of these voices dominating the others, cried in tones filled with rage: "Save yourself, save yourself!" At the sound of this exclamation which resembled a threat, the lady lifted her head and frowned as she gazed in the direction of the river. Upon this simple movement the terrified voices fled in all directions. This new apparition had intensified the emotion as well as the curiosity of the people of Lourdes.

Every one knew that Bernadette had promised to return to the Grotto for a fortnight. As a result, the following day, Saturday, as she arrived at 6.30 A. M. in company with her mother, already five hundred persons were there to greet her. Instantly a religious silence spreads over the multitude. Bernadette, apparently unaffected by this concourse of people, as if she had been all alone, knelt and began the recitation of her rosary. After a few short moments the ecstasy was on, a reproduction of yesterday's characteristics. At times her lips indicate that she is speaking, then again she listens. All can readily understand, though they hear nothing, that a conversation is taking place between the child and the apparition; no one grasps anything tangible, yet all can see upon Bernadette's transfigured countenance the reflection of a Divine Light. That the lady is there before her none can deny, any more than one denies the presence of the sun, when though he does not see it, he witnesses its rays.

Up to the present time, in each of the apparitions, everything transpired solely between the lady and the child without even the slightest suggestion of anything foreign to the visionary herself; a sort of supernatural education which the Celestial Lady inculcated by degrees. The first apparition was purely a presentation; in the second and third intimacy is engendered with confidence; in the fourth the lady exercises her sovereign power when, with one glance, she puts to flight the powers of darkness; and finally, in the fifth apparition, she teaches her young protégée how to pray for her own personal needs. "She was kind enough," said Bernadette, "to teach me, word by word, a prayer particularly and most especially intended for me." What was that prayer? Nobody knows; the young girl has declared that she did not feel authorized to make it public. . . . Let us gather nevertheless from this fact the all important lesson that our personal prayers are necessary to obtain the graces we are most in need of in working out our sanctification and salvation. But it isn't for Bernadette's advantage alone that the lady appears to her; her views are broader and more comprehensive. She begins by preparing the one she has chosen as her instrument, her intermediary for the works of mercy she has come to accomplish on earth. Each of the succeeding apparitions will reveal new progress, and the Heavenly Teacher will soon begin to place her pupil in her maternal confidence.

INVOCATION

Hail, Mary.

"O sweet Mother of Jesus, how grateful we are to thee for having brought before us the greatest lesson of the gospel, the necessity of prayer. Grant us the grace of understanding it so well, and practicing it so faithfully, that we may always find in prayer, with its indispensable help, the happiness and consolation of our lives.

"Our Lady of Lourdes, pray for us."

CHAPTER VI

SIXTH APPARITION

Dr. Dozous—"Pray for Sinners"
Procurator and Commissary

ON Sunday, long before sunrise, a most unique spectacle greeted the eye: In the vicinity of the Grotto, in the adjoining fields, on the banks of the Gave, in the crevices of the rocks, in every conceivable nook and corner, an immense throng thousands in number had gathered from Lourdes and its surroundings that they might get a glimpse of the visionary.

In this vast concourse of people were noticed a certain number of Lourdes's most representative citizens; amongst others let us mention most particularly Dr. Dozous, a learned and judicious doctor in medicine, highly esteemed in Lourdes, but wholly indifferent in matters of religion. He discounted all supernatural intervention and believed in science only. For him Bernadette's case was nothing more than the manifestations of one of those odd diseases of the neuropathic order; and now as the occasion for a close-up observation presented itself he was happy to avail himself of the opportunity. Yes, he will study this phenomenon so thoroughly that he will soon become one of the most authorized as well as one of the most convinced witnesses of the Divine Apparition. In this very Grotto of Lourdes, his loyal mind will be opened to the light

of faith, his heart to a most ardent devotion to the
Immaculate Mary; by his words and writings he will
champion her cause until the very end of his life.

Bernadette, accompanied by a member of her family, arrived, modest and simple as usual. At her approach the throng respectfully opened a lane through
which she passed. On arriving at the Grotto she knelt
and reverently began the recitation of her rosary, her
eyes in the meantime fixed upon the opening just over
the rosebush. One of the bystanders having offered
her a lighted candle, she took it and held it in her
right hand. Presently, the ordinary signs of her ecstasies told the multitude that the Celestial Apparition
was there. Strangely enough, notwithstanding the fact
that her attention was entirely absorbed in the contemplation of her august visitor, she was partly conscious of what was happening about her. For instance,
it occurred frequently that her candle was extinguished
by a gust of wind and each time she extended her arm
to have it relighted. Doctor Dozous took a position
at her side and felt her pulse; she apparently paid no
attention to him. Since then the learned doctor has
published a detailed account of his observations in his
book entitled: "The Grotto of Lourdes." His testimony as one may well imagine, has a most important
bearing upon this marvelous affair. We quote from
the following passage, relative to the present incident:

"The pulse was normal, regular,—the respiration
easy; nothing in the young girl seemed to indicate

nervousness, or over-excitement. Upon releasing her arm she rose and proceeded a trifle in the direction of the Grotto. Presently I noticed that her features which up to this moment reflected the most genuine happiness, became saddened; two tears fell from her eyes and rolled down her cheeks. This sudden change on her countenance somewhat puzzled me. At the end of her prayers, and after the mysterious lady had disappeared, I asked her what had taken place during this long period; she answered: 'The lady, as she momentarily withdrew her attention from me, cast a glance over and above my head into the distance. She again looked in my direction and as I asked her why she appeared so sad, she replied: *Pray for sinners!* I was quickly reassured by the expression of kindness which reappeared on her countenance and immediately she vanished.' At the close of this apparition," continues Dr. Dozous, "where the people had been overwhelmed with emotion, Bernadette, always simple and modest in her demeanor, returned to her home."

The chief characteristic of the sixth apparition is found in these words: *"Pray for sinners!"* It is the first mission entrusted to Bernadette; it is also the most important of all the works performed at Lourdes. All that is accomplished there, whether by God's intervention or by man, converges primarily to the conversion of sinners.

How shall we ever know the number of souls that have returned to the path of righteousness, either through Lourdes or the wonders that are performed there! Think of the conversion of so many unbelievers, freethinkers, heretics, and dissenters! How admirably Mary exemplifies one of her most beloved titles: Refuge of Sinners! To interest one's self in this work, the greatest of all, since it is the object of the Redemption, is to respond to Mary's most cherished ideals and to merit her favors.

From this day the civil authorities began to concern themselves with these recent events, for most undeniably, the city and the region thereabouts were all agitation. The mayor, Mr. Anselme Lacadé, a notary public, the imperial procurator, Mr. Jacques Dutour, and the commissary of police, Mr. Dominique Jacomet, met at the city hall on this particular Sunday morning to deliberate upon just how to cope with the situation. Not one of these men believed in the supernatural; they rather suspected in all these stories of the Grotto an unhealthy, if not a guilty cause. They decided that henceforth all manifestations or meetings should be forbidden, avoiding at the same time, all that would tend to irritate the public.

First of all, Bernadette was to be asked, without violence, not to return to the Grotto. The procurator himself having assumed this duty, ordered the young girl to be brought before him. In vain did he try persuasion, in vain did he resort to threat. "Promise me," as he brought the interview to a close, "that you will not return to Massabielle."

"Sir, I cannot promise that," answered Bernadette.

"Is this your last word?"

"Yes, sir."

"Then go,—we will see."

For the procurator this meant a signal defeat which he did not hesitate to admit in his report. The commissary, a crafty individual, figured that he would fare a little better, so he proceeded to the church and waited for Bernadette at the close of Vespers. A guard who accompanied him pointed her out as she emerged from the building in company with her Aunt Lucille. He accosted her, as if by accident, and bade her accompany him to his office. The child, undisturbed, obeyed the magistrate whilst her aunt hurried home to acquaint the family with the cause of her delay.

The session was long, the cross-examination insidious, and replete with danger. At the outset, a witness entered the room; this was Mr. Estrade, the registrar, who in his book, "The Apparitions at Lourdes," has given a detailed account of the interview. The commissary made use of all the cunning common to his position as police officer: flatteries, promises, threats,— but all in vain. This poor ignorant child who had nothing to conceal answered straightforwardly; she carefully avoided the traps which the wily magistrate had set for her, correcting, one after the other, his willful errors and his insidious allegations which were intended to confuse her and to make her contradict herself. All attempts having failed, the commissary was at a loss to know just what to do, when suddenly

Bernadette's father entered the room. Seizing the opportunity, the official resolved to use this good man as an instrument to obtain his end. He went so far as to threaten to arrest him and to imprison his daughter. François Soubirous, trembling with fright, promised everything and thereupon, left with Bernadette.

How these officials exemplified the ideas of their times! They repudiated the supernatural in the name of science. Poor science, to be made the slave of pride and scepticism! What nonsense! as if the supernatural, the intervention of God in the government of a world created by Him, which is called Providence, was not a necessary consequence of creation! Simply a question of common sense. God cannot become indifferent to His works, which derive from Him (as says St. Paul) their life, their activity, their very existence. This is one of the greatest lessons given by the Blessed Virgin to a foolish age. The entire story of Lourdes is nothing else but the brilliant confirmation of the supernatural seconded by miracles, and the lamentable failure of false science.

INVOCATION

Hail, Mary.

"O Mary, Mother of our Redeemer, how beautiful and instructive is thy compassion for sinners. It tells us how sin was responsible for the Passion and Death of thy Divine Son,—how sin to-day renders useless so many sufferings and humiliations,—how it casts into hell so many souls who spurn the benefits of the Redeemer. Inspire us with a deep horror for sin, as well as with a tender and most efficacious mercy for sinners.

"Our Lady of Lourdes, pray for us."

CHAPTER VII

FIRST DECEPTION AND SEVENTH APPARITION

*Strange Obstacle—The Gendarmes
At the Commissary's—Mr. Estrade*

THE following day Bernadette, through a sense of obedience, refrained from going to the Grotto. Sadly she wended her way to school, whence she returned at the noon hour without ever deviating from her path. After dinner, in all docility, she returned to her class; her heart and her every thought were at Massabielle, but duty ruled over her desires.

As she approached the hospice where the poor attended the Sisters' classes, she suddenly came to a halt, for there stood before her an invisible barrier which she repeatedly, but vainly attempted to pass. Troubled by this impediment, which appeared so unnatural, the poor disconsolate child wondered what might be the cause. Would it not be her unfaithfulness to the promise she had made the lady? And yet, on the other hand, she would be disobeying. What cruel perplexity! And all this time her actions were being secretly scrutinized by people as astonished as they were interested; these were officers from the neighboring barracks appointed by the commissary to shadow her every movement. After a fresh attempt to break down this barrier, she turned suddenly, as if commanded by some mysterious force, and with rapid strides she started in the direction of Massabielle. She was not disobeying, as a will foreign to her own seemed to command her; invisible angels, undoubtedly, directed her footsteps. But presently, a few officers joined her, and gruffly asked her where she was going. "I am on my way to the Grotto," she answered, without even stopping or turning her head. And these brave military men, on special duty, followed her. Let it be said that their deportment on the way was most proper and respectful; they were there to observe only, in order to file a report. How little this company seemed to trouble Bernadette, for, absolutely calm and self-possessed, she walked quietly along in the direction of the Grotto.

That morning, as predicted, a great concourse of people had gathered at Massabielle, so we may well imagine their keen disappointment over Bernadette's absence. After hours of patient waiting the multitude gradually began to disperse. And still the Grotto was never without some visitors; from all sides, people came to visit the scene of the apparitions,—many to offer up prayers. The pilgrimage to Lourdes had begun, never to be discontinued.

The arrival of Bernadette at this particular hour of the day soon attracted a considerable number of people. The young girl at once knelt in prayerful attitude as she had always done before. All was perfectly silent about her.   A long period elapsed and no change came over her features; the apparition did not occur.   What a deception for the poor child, so sorely tried since the previous day, so disturbed by incidents and contradictions which here on earth govern things Divine; she was given on this day her first lesson.   The education of her new-born soul was accentuated by the privation of her daily joys and consolations, by her apparent abandonment in the midst of the agonies and sorrows which overwhelmed her.

With a saddened heart she rose and was about to depart when suddenly, her mother arrived.   Bernadette related to her in detail all that had happened on the way to school and how she had felt herself drawn to the Grotto.   Together they entered the Savy mill, followed by a number of ladies.   Conspicuous among these was Mlle. Estrade, sister of the registrar, whom we met yesterday at Bernadette's interrogatory in the commissary's office.   None of these ladies had ever met either Bernadette or her mother.   A conversation ensued during which Mme. Soubirous told them what tribulations and torments these events were causing her family; that after all both her husband and herself would discontinue all opposition,—for they fully realized that the sincerity and truthfulness of their child was such that they could no longer doubt the genuineness of the apparitions.

In the city a diversity of impressions prevailed. Those who maintained that the events at the Grotto

MR. J. B. ESTRADE
One of the most important witnesses of the apparitions

were nothing else but folly, hallucination, or even a well-conceived plan of mystification or fraud, were jubilant over the recent discomfiture. They congratulated the capable commissary for having found the proper means of putting an end to all these ridiculous stories. Others, and they were in the majority, did not hesitate to see in these new developments another astounding proof of the child's sincerity. The commissary terribly annoyed at finding his orders thus violated, and having heard that the girl's father had withdrawn his opposition, sent for all three, father, mother, and daughter, and reiterated his former threats; but this time he spoke to people of a much different disposition.

"My daughter has never lied," retorted François Soubirous, "and if God and the Virgin Mary call her, we cannot oppose ourselves.—God would punish us for so doing."

"Those are all silly stories," replied the terrible functionary, "and I will have you all cast in prison, if your daughter persists in exciting the people with all this foolishness."

"But, Sir," cried out Bernadette, "I go there to pray all alone, I ask no one to follow me, and if so many people come before and after me, it is not my fault."

The commissary, absolutely disconcerted, had nothing to reply and not the tiniest bit of law to invoke; that is what exasperated him.

The following day, Tuesday, February 23, a vast throng assembled at the Grotto. Mr. Estrade, acceding

to the entreaties of his sister, finally accompanied her.
Rather shy at finding himself there,—for he belonged
to the group of unbelievers, his mind was set at ease as
he came in contact with many gentlemen from the city;
among others, Dr. Dozous, lawyer Dufo, the commander of the fortress, and Mr. De La Fitte, former
commissary of stores and proprietor of these grounds.

Herewith is given Mr. Estrade's description of the
day's events: "At about six o'clock in the morning, I
arrived at the Grotto; many women were already there,
praying on their knees; and truly, I could hardly refrain from laughing at the sight of this simple faith
on the part of these poor Christians.   After a few
moments a confused sound spread over the assembly,—
it was whispered that the child was on her way.   Immediately a lane was opened and Bernadette appeared.
We men, using our elbows, pushed the weaker ones
aside and drew up close to the girl.   From this moment
Bernadette had to be truly careful, for our eyes were
focussed upon her.   She knelt, took her rosary in hand
and bowed profoundly; all her movements were natural and devoid of constraint.

"Whilst she was praying, suddenly, as if a streak of
lightning had struck her, she bounded with admiration
and appeared to enter into a new life.   Her eyes
glistened brilliantly, an angelic smile covered her lips,
and an indefinable grace permeated her entire person.
Bernadette was no longer Bernadette.   It was there

that we men, we haughty men, removed our hats and bowed reverently in imitation of the most humble women. The hour of reasoning had passed,—we were now witnessing a scene from Heaven.

"Soon the visionary assumed the attitude of one listening; her gestures and her countenance bespoke every phase of a conversation. Now serious, now again smiling, she assented, by a nod of her head, or appeared to interrogate. The ecstasy lasted about one hour. Near the close of the apparition the child crept upon her knees to a spot just below the rosebush, kissed the earth, and then without rising, returned to her position. Her features once more became resplendent, and, gradually they resumed their natural aspect, always amiable though rustic.

"After such a scene," continues Mr. Estrade, "I felt as one who has just emerged from a trance. I could not control my emotion, and a world of thoughts besieged my soul. The lady of the Grotto may have tried in vain to conceal herself,—I felt her presence nevertheless, and I was convinced that her maternal gaze had rested upon my person. Oh! most solemn hour of my life! I became almost delirious at the thought that I, the man of conceit and of a thousand mockeries, had been admitted to a position close to the Queen of Heaven! Asked to disclose what the lady had told her, Bernadette said that she had been given three secrets, but for herself alone. All that could be done to induce the child to reveal them failed utterly, and Bernadette has carried them with her to the grave." ("Les Apparitions de Lourdes," by Mr. Estrade.)

INVOCATION

Hail, Mary.

"O Mary, it is through the thorny path of sorrows and contradictions that thou guidest, step by step, thy pupil. Grant us the grace of assimilating for ourselves this most precious lesson,—that we may better understand the words of thy Son: 'If one wishes to become My disciple, let him take up his cross and follow Me.'

"Our Lady of Lourdes, pray for us."

CHAPTER VIII

EIGHTH APPARITION

*"Penance, penance, penance!"—And again
The Gendarmes*

OUR story now takes us to Wednesday, February 24. Without wishing to delve into the secrets of God, or to understand the mysterious revelations which were made to Bernadette on the preceding day, can we not suppose that their object was to prepare the young girl for the solemn messages she was soon to receive? Nothing was more necessary to her than humility,— and this great virtue was to become all the more prominent in this child, by reason of the publicity and popularity her mission was to bring her,—to say nothing of the many perilous homages. It was expedient that she guard herself against all sentiments of pride to which she was to be inevitably exposed. Poor girl, taken from so lowly a position and exalted to so high a station, chosen by the Queen of Heaven to become her intermediary and her representative before the universe! But the Blessed Virgin who had constituted herself her teacher, saw to it that she was sufficiently protected against such a danger. The virtues of humility and simplicity, of which Mary had been such an eminent model, never suffered an iota in Bernadette's heart, and to the last moment of her existence, they will remain her cherished standard, her personal characteristic.

Here she is at her customary hour of the morning, kneeling before the Grotto upon the particular spot she had selected, and which was always held in reverence by the people. On that day the multitude had increased notably, due, no doubt, to the cruel vexations the poor child was made to endure. After a few moments of prayer, the ineffable Beauty, whose return she craved, revealed herself to her eyes once more and enraptured her completely. From the child's demeanor, one could understand that a conversation was going on between the two. But suddenly her features give way to sadness, her eyes become moistened and abundant tears roll down her cheeks. Presently she rises and slowly ascends the grade that leads to the rock, kneeling and prostrating herself at each step, and then kissing the earth.

Let us admire how the Blessed Virgin, in order to teach her humility, compels her to multiply exterior acts of this virtue. As we proceed we shall come across many other examples.

Upon reaching the cliff Bernadette prostrates herself once more; then looking up at the apparition she rises to her feet as if to draw herself closer to it. For a moment she listens,—then turning towards the people, in a voice choked with sobs, she shouts this triple cry: "Penance! penance! penance!" All understood that, in imitation of the echo, she simply repeated the words she had heard, and which she had been commanded to transmit to the multitude.

It would be impossible to describe the effect produced by this scene upon the people. All eyes were filled with tears; everybody understood that this appeal to penance was the natural outcome of the pressing invitation of a few days ago to pray for sinners.

Reparation must naturally follow sin; we owe it to God on account of our personal offenses; it is the price of our salvation. "Unless you do penance," says our Lord, "you will all perish." We also owe it to God for the sins of our neighbors. There exists between all men, for good and for evil, a certain solidarity whose consequences and responsibilities, in a measure, we share. Have not all the saints been penitents, forgivers? Expiation is an integral part of the essence of Christian life. Alas! this law of penance has never been so despised as during this corrupt century of ours. The Blessed Virgin came to remind us of it. This was the first message to Bernadette; already it has been reëchoed throughout the world, and has given rise to many salutary reparations.

Bernadette had, in the meantime, returned to her position and her features had once more resumed their ecstatic beauty, when an incident occurred that filled all hearts with indignation: Two gendarmes rushed madly into the Grotto, crying: "Room, room!" One of the two, a quarter-master of cavalry, approached the young girl arrogantly, saying: "Well, what are you doing there, you little comedienne?"   Bernadette unmoved, as if she had heard nothing, continued her colloquy with the vision, whilst the gendarme, absolutely stupefied and evidently much embarrassed with his awkward rôle, did his best to appear natural, as he shouted the insulting irony: "And to think that all this foolishness occurs in this nineteenth century!" This was too much; a most disquieting murmur arose from the multitude and a number of workmen rushed forward ready to intervene.   Nothing more was required to make the two intruders understand that they themselves had committed a blunder,—to say nothing of a supreme impropriety.   As a result, low cowardice having replaced their arrogance, they hastened away without uttering another word.

Shortly afterwards, Bernadette, arm in arm with her aunt, returned to her home, whilst the multitude, as it dispersed, commented upon the various phases of the sensational events.

God, in His allpowerfulness, makes use of obstacles to further His ends.   We will see, in subsequent chapters, that the intervention of the public authorities, far from hindering the works of Lourdes, helped materially, inasmuch as they gave them—First, more publicity by their opposition at the outset, and—Second, a more authentic credit by the control which these same authorities attributed to them.

Is it not also this same intervention which proved without the shadow of a doubt, to the Jews of Jerusalem the reality of Christ's resurrection of which Pilate's soldiers were the principal and official witnesses? Thus it is that the opposition on the part of the authorities of Lourdes furnished a solid proof that all the events there were true, sincere, and supernatural.

INVOCATION

Hail, Mary.

"O Mary, another great lesson which our cowardice makes us too often forget, the necessity of penance. We thank thee, O good Mother, for having brought it to our minds. Grant us the grace of so conforming our lives to it, that our sins forgotten and atoned for, be not imputed to us when we appear before our Sovereign Judge.

"Our Lady of Lourdes, pray for us."

CHAPTER IX

NINTH APPARITION

"Go drink, and cleanse yourself at the Fountain"

OF all the apparitions of the Blessed Virgin to Bernadette, the one that we are about to describe is one of the most important by reason of its effects. For the child and the immense concourse of people, it meant a series of disconcerting trials. If poor Bernadette had not possessed such profound humility, how her pride would have suffered! Truly, the good Virgin was leading her pupil through a path strewn with thorns.

This is how Mr. Estrade, an eye witness, relates the strange scenes as they were enacted on Thursday morning, February 25:

"She was there under my gaze in her angelic pose when, after a few moments of meditation, she rose and started towards the Grotto. She brushed aside the eglantine branches, and continued beyond the bush underneath the cliff where she stooped and kissed the earth; shortly after, she returned to her position and having recollected herself, she again fell into ecstasy. At the end of the second or third decade of her beads she rose once more and appeared somewhat embarrassed; hesitatingly, she turned towards the Gave and advanced two or three steps in that direction. But behold! she stopped abruptly, looked behind as though someone had called her, and listened to words that seemed to come from the cliff. She made a sign in the affirmative, resumed her gait,—not in the direction of the Gave, but towards the Grotto, at the left angle of the excavation. At a point about three-quarters of the way up the incline, she stopped and looked about in wonderment; she lifted her head as if to question the lady, and then, resolutely, she bent over and started to scratch the earth. The small cavity in the ground instantly filled with water. After a short interval she stooped, drank of the same and bathed her face in it; she also plucked a blade of glass that grew nearby and carried it to her mouth.

"All the spectators followed the different phases of this bewildering scene with a sense of anguish and evident stupor. When the child rose to regain her customary place, her face still showed the effects of the muddy water. At this aspect a cry of deception and pity fell from all lips: 'Bernadette is no longer herself, the poor child has lost her head!' She returned to her position, apparently unmoved, unmindful of the many exclamations which resounded in her ears. After wiping her face, now happier than ever, an ecstatic smile on her lips, she resumed the contemplation of the Heavenly Vision. Quiet and recollected she continued her delectation in prayer, under the eyes of the one she loved. Presently, at seven o'clock, the hour at which the apparition generally came to an end, she made the sign of the cross and returned to the city, conversing on her way with that air of confidence so becoming to her. To all questions relative to her actions at the Grotto, all of which appeared so strange, she replied: 'Whilst I was praying, the lady said to me in an amiable but serious tone of voice: "Go to the fountain, drink and cleanse yourself." As I was ignorant of the whereabouts of this fountain,—and as, after all, it mattered little, I proceeded towards the Gave. The lady called me back, and with a movement of her finger, she bade me go to the Grotto, on the left; I obeyed, but I saw no water. Not knowing where to find any I began scratching the ground and water came. I allowed it to settle for a while, then I drank of it and bathed my face as ordered.' 'You also ate a blade of grass, and why?' 'I do not know;—the lady urged me to it through some hidden force.' " Such is the account given by Mr. Estrade.

Another witness who also had been a close observer and who in like manner has published his observations, Dr. Dozous, whom we have already met, took pains before leaving the Grotto, to examine the ground very carefully. He asserts that everywhere the earth was perfectly dry, except the spot that had been scratched by Bernadette, and from which water had gushed forth.

This spring which at first produced but a tiny thread of water, increased gradually; the following day it had attained the size of a finger, and a few days later that of a child's arm; in a short time it had reached extraordinary proportions. From that period the flow of water has been constant and, furthermore, it has never diminished in volume. Fifteen faucets dispense it to the pilgrims who drink it and use it for diverse purposes; it is also brought to nine different bathing apartments for the use of the sick. Its daily output is 26,840 gallons or 18 gallons a minute.

Following the disconcerting scenes of the ninth apparition, the enemies had noisily triumphed; but this was short-lived, as they were soon silenced by this most unheard-of and most irrefutable fact which had all the characteristics of a miracle. One thing certain, nobody had ever known of the existence of a spring at the Grotto. It matters little if it came from a subterranean body of water, for the circumstances surrounding its appearance were certainly not natural. And in this lies the miracle.

Such is the origin of the celebrated water of Lourdes, which has since been distributed in vast quantities to the four corners of the globe; it has also been an incontestable instrument to numerous cures.

The actions of Bernadette may have appeared strange to those who witnessed them, simply because they failed to understand the motive and the end. But for us what precious lessons are contained in the scene we have just contemplated! Ordinarily, water serves a double purpose,—it purifies and it quenches thirst. Under this double aspect it often symbolizes the sacrament of Penance: "Drink and cleanse yourself at the fountain," said Mary to the young girl; not in the river, as Bernadette had supposed at first, (the river with its noisy and disorderly onrush represents the world). The water which alleviates thirst and purifies souls represents that pure water of which our Lord spoke to the Samaritan woman at Jacob's well and which should be drawn from a mysterious fountain; this is the purifying water of grace which is obtained only through hardships and labor. To become purified of our faults one must submit to the hardships of penance together with the humiliations of the sacrament:—confession, contrition, and satisfaction. By this means the soul is cleansed of its stains and strengthened by the divine water of grace. This wonderful effect of the sacrament of Penance is admirably represented in the cures wrought, in a great measure, by the use of the water which the Blessed Virgin commanded to spring from the ground at the touch of Bernadette's hand.

INVOCATION

Hail, Mary.

"O Mary, Mother of divine grace, what a precious gift thou hast made us in this fountain of pure water, which, at thy bidding, sprang from the bosom of the earth, and of which thy word: 'Go drink, and cleanse yourself' means so much to us all! Under thy guidance may we become more zealous in drinking and cleansing ourselves at the salutary fountains of the sacraments.

"Our Lady of Lourdes, pray for us."

CHAPTER X

TENTH APPARITION

"You will kiss the earth for Sinners"
Louis Bourriette

THE incidents connected with the fountain at the Grotto resounded throughout the entire region. From the most distant points of the province came multitudes of people, all anxious to be present at the now famous cliffs the following day. At early dawn from five to six thousand persons had already gathered in the vicinity of the Grotto. Bernadette, on arriving, ascended the grade that led to the fountain; she knelt, made the sign of the cross with dignity, and stooped for a handful of water. After drinking a little, she bathed her face, wiping it with her apron instead of a towel. Following this ceremony she went and knelt at her customary spot. It was not long before her countenance reflected the beauty of the Heavenly Apparition. Presently, as it had occurred at the eighth apparition, a tone of sadness replaced her angelic smile and tears trickled down her cheeks. Rising from her place she advanced a few steps in the direction of the cliff, prostrated herself and kissed the earth with great fervor. Rising instantly, and turning towards the multitude, with a sign of the hand she bade them imitate her. And this vast concourse of people, without hesitation, obeyed the child's command,—for everybody felt that she was acting upon orders from the most exalted of sovereigns after God Himself. Every knee was bended, every lip kissed the earth. What a spectacle! Many unbelievers mixed in the throng, their eyes filled with tears, performed most astonishingly this act of humiliation and penance. We may well surmise that at this particular moment many rebellious hearts received the first germs of conversion.

What had taken place in this secret colloquy between the child and her Heavenly Visitor? The lady had told her: "You will kiss the earth for sinners." Here then is the great preoccupation of one who is at the same time Mother of the Redeemer, and, by adoption, Mother of the redeemed sinners. She craves the salvation of sinners, and she constantly refers to the means of obtaining it,—humility and penance. And such was the characteristic note of the tenth apparition.

Let us revert to the water of the fountain which the people, in their enthusiasm, had already styled miraculous.

There lived at Lourdes a poor laborer, well known throughout the city, by the name of Louis Bourriette. He was a quarryman, one employed at extracting marble from the quarries which, by the way, abound in this region. Twenty years previously he had been the victim of a terrible accident; as a result of a badly timed explosion, his right eye had been half crushed by a chip of stone; at the same time, his brother,

DR. DOZOUS
One of the chief witnesses of the
apparitions

LOUIS BOURRIETTE
The first invalid to be cured by means
of the miraculous water

MR. DOMINIQUE JACOMET
Commissary of Police

DR. G. BOISSARIE
Chief of the Medical Clinic at Lourdes
(1892 - 1917)

Joseph, was killed at his side. Notwithstanding all the efforts of science nothing could be done to restore the use of the affected organ. A faint light is all that the eye could discern, so much so, that in closing the left eye he could not distinguish a man from a tree. As soon as he heard of this new fountain at the Grotto, he despatched his daughter to go and bring him some of the water. It was still soiled and muddy. Bourriette, after having made the sign of the cross, took a little of it and rubbed the eye which had been useless for so many years. He instantly shrieked with joy for he was regaining his sight. He continued to pray and to rub the eye and, by and by, all objects were clearly visible to him. The following day, perceiving Dr. Dozous on the city square, he rushes to him triumphantly, crying:

"I am cured!"

"Impossible," answered the doctor, "your case is hopeless; the treatment which I prescribed to you has for sole object the alleviation of your sufferings but it cannot restore the use of your eye."

"You are not the one who cured me," cried the man with emotion, "it is the Blessed Virgin of the Grotto."

The man of human science shrugged his shoulders, and seizing a note book he wrote a few lines with a pencil; then, putting his hand upon Bourriette's left eye he placed the phrase he had just written before the affected organ. With an air of triumphant defiance the eminent doctor said: "If you can read this, I will believe you." Immediately, with a strong voice and without the slightest hesitation, Bourriette read the following words: "Bourriette has an incurable amaurosis and he will never recover." The doctor was as much astounded as if a thunderbolt had crashed at his feet; he was a man of science, but also a man of conscience, and he did not hesitate to acknowledge in this sudden cure of an incurable affliction, the intervention of a superior power. "I cannot deny," said he; "it is a miracle, a real miracle; it overpowers me,—yet one has to submit before such evidence." Doctor Vergez of Tarbes, professor at the Faculty of Medicine of Montpellier, and a doctor of renown at the Baths of Barèges, having been called to give his opinion of this particular case, did not hesitate in handing down a detailed report, to call it a miracle.

Other cures no less surprising were recorded in the city in a short space of time; all were scrupulously authenticated and officially acknowledged by means of medical certificates.

Bourriette's cure caused a tremendous sensation in Lourdes; it threw the faction of unbelievers in an uproar,—but the vast majority of the people proclaimed with joy and gratitude a supernatural intervention, that is,—a miracle.

In the corporation to which Bourriette belonged this wonderful event created unbounded enthusiasm. During the evening of this same day, a number of quarrymen returning from their work, proceeded with their tools to Massabielle and chiselled in the rock a new path in order to facilitate the approach to the Grotto. Before the cavity of the fountain they placed a wooden trough, under which they dug a small oval-shaped reservoir of twenty inches in depth and about the size of a child's cradle. We will find that this corporation of quarrymen did not stop with this first act of gratitude.

INVOCATION

Hail, Mary.

"O holy Virgin, mirror of justice, in this tenth apparition, in ordering Bernadette to kiss the earth for the sinners, thou remindest us that mortification and humility are necessary to the expiation of sin,—the fruit of pride and sensuality; ask God for us, poor sinners, the grace of understanding this great lesson, and to courageously put it into practice.

"Our Lady of Lourdes, pray for us."

CHAPTER XI

ELEVENTH APPARITION

"Go and tell the Priests . . ."
The Pastor of Lourdes

SATURDAY, February 27, as on all previous days, a very large gathering of people had preceded Bernadette at the Grotto. On the arrival of the visionary the same phenomena were enacted, and by her transfiguration one could easily perceive that the apparition was taking place. For the people there was nothing out of the ordinary; yet the colloquy between the lady and the privileged child lasted longer than usual. At the close of the ecstasy, after Bernadette had returned home, she announced to her mother that the lady had given her the following message for the Pastor of Lourdes: "Go and tell the priests that I want a chapel erected here." The thought of calling at the rectory was, for the timid child, a matter of much concern; yet in a spirit of obedience, she made up her mind to go.

Undoubtedly it must have been noted, not without some astonishment, that up to the present time the clergy had been eliminated from this whole affair, which, for a fortnight, had so passionately captivated the attention of the people. This abstention on their part in a matter so intimately connected with religion was not the result of indifference but rather of wise precaution. The Pastor of Lourdes as well as his three assistants had managed from the start to keep well posted upon all the incidents relative to the Grotto, but they waited prudently before mixing in the affair, fully convinced that if it were necessary, Divine Providence would call them in time.

The parish of Lourdes, the seat of a deanery, was governed by a priest of high merit,—Abbé Peyramale, a man of staunch faith, profound piety, and austere habits. He enjoyed universal esteem and affection and for this reason his authority over the people was perfect. Physically, he was tall, of energetic features, and quite stern in appearance; yet in his dealings with his people he was familiar, affable, and easy of access. Bernadette had never spoken to him, having returned to Lourdes as we recall, but a few weeks previously in order that she might prepare for her first communion. She attended both the Sisters' school and the catechism classes under the supervision of Abbé Pomian, chaplain of the hospice. She therefore called at the rectory.

The parish house stood at the farther end of a terrace where Abbé Peyramale was occupied reciting his breviary. The little girl, modest and timid, went directly to him. The priest, interrupting his prayer for a moment, asked her who she was and what she wanted. "I am Bernadette Soubirous," answered the child.

"Ah! it is you," replied the Pastor, with some severity, "people are circulating strange stories on your account, my poor child; follow me inside." He thereupon led the way into the parlor. "Well now, what do you want?"

"The lady of the Grotto has given me a message,— that of telling the priests that she wants a chapel erected at Massabielle and that is why I came to see you."

"What about that lady that you speak of," replied the Pastor, feigning ignorance of the whole story?

"It is a beautiful lady who appears to me on the cliff of Massabielle."

"Yes, but who is this lady? Does she live here in Lourdes? Do you know her?"

"She is not from Lourdes, I do not know her."

"And you accept from a person whom you do not know a message such as this?"

"Oh, but, M. l'Abbé, the lady who sends me here does not resemble other ladies."

"What do you mean?"

"I mean that she is handsome as one is, I suppose, in Heaven."

"And you have never asked this lady's name?"

"Yes, I have,—but when I do she lowers her head, smiles, but does not answer."

"She is therefore dumb?"

"Oh! no, for we converse together every day; if she were dumb she could not have told me to come and see you."

"At least, tell me how you came to meet her."

The priest having seated himself, bade the young girl to do likewise. Bernadette calmly and truthfully began the narrative of all she had seen and heard at the Grotto from the first apparition. As the child unfolded her story, the good Pastor felt that his prejudices vanished one by one. Accustomed to read the human heart, he admired secretly the sincerity of this simple child unwinding, in her rustic dialect, events as marvelous as could be conceived, given the condition of her untrained mind. Through those limpid eyes, back of that truthful countenance, he could discern the wonderful innocence of this privileged soul. Have we not already noticed that even unbelievers have felt this same influence? The priest's firmness, nevertheless, held his secret emotion in check, and he was able to maintain before the child his sceptic appearance. In the interests of the truth he resolved to put her to a test.

Continuing with a gruff voice: "And you maintain that the lady gave you a message to tell the priests that she wishes to have a chapel erected at Massabielle?"

"Yes, M. le Curé."

"But can't you see that the lady wished to make fun of you? If a lady of the city had asked you a similar favor would you have listened to her?"

"Oh, but there is a vast difference between the ladies of the city and the one that I see!"

"Yes, there is quite a difference! Think of it!—a woman who has no name, whom nobody knows whence she comes, who appears on the cliff,—and barefooted, —can such a woman be considered seriously? My dear girl, I fear that you have fallen a victim to an illusion."

Bernadette did not answer. A few moments of silence followed, during which the Pastor walked excitedly back and forth in the parlor. Returning to Bernadette, he said to her: "Go and tell the lady who sent you here that the Pastor of Lourdes has not the habit of dealing with people he doesn't know. In the first place, she must give her name and prove that she has a right to it; if the lady insists upon the erection of a chapel, she will understand the import of my words; if she doesn't understand, tell her that she can dispense with sending any more messages to the parish." With these words the Pastor dismissed Bernadette who left somewhat embarrassed, but neither discouraged nor disquieted. She knew full well that her mission was divine, and that it would succeed notwithstanding all the contradictions.

The good Curé's actions may savor of too much severity but they were actuated by a sense of prudence. If the priests had become interested in the matter, some would have accused them of being the instigators of the whole affair, of planning the acts and drilling the actors. Their wise reserve precluded the possibility of such an insinuation. His Lordship, the Bishop of Tarbes, highly commended this line of conduct, and thereupon ordered all his priests to keep aloof.

ABBÉ PEYRAMALE
Bernadette's Pastor at Lourdes

INVOCATION

Hail, Mary.

"O Mary, Virgin most wise, man, in his pride, is oftentimes inclined to independence and contempt of authority. In the Church of Christ this authority reposes in the priesthood, divine magistracy instituted by her Founder. To us all thou recallest this fundamental rule when thou didst despatch thy messenger to submit thy order to the legitimate pastors. Grant us the grace of perfect obedience to those to whom is confided the government of our souls.

"Our Lady of Lourdes, pray for us."

CHAPTER XII

TWELFTH AND THIRTEENTH APPARITIONS
The Soldiers—The Rosary

DAYS were now too short to satisfy the devotion and curiosity of the multitudes. The Grotto was always filled, even at night; candles burned continually, and the strains of hymns and litanies reëchoed without interruption. Although the lady had not as yet divulged her name, everybody felt that it was none other than the august Virgin Mary.

Sunday morning, February 28, an enormous concourse of people had gathered,—from Bigorre and Béarn,—city people, country folks, mountaineers,—all were massed between the Gave and the now famous cliff. As Bernadette arrived, this compact throng, religiously silent, made way for her. In keeping with the Lord's day, the young girl is neatly attired in her Sunday garments; she is accompanied by her Aunt Lucille. The child kneels and prays and after a few brief moments the ordinary signs of the mysterious interview are flashed upon her features. No one but Bernadette sees the lady, but all are filled with her presence. The interview was long, consisting mainly of the recitation of the beads, the kissing of the earth, and the conversation, the details of which have been kept a secret. The spectators who gazed at the visionary prayed with her, knelt and kissed the earth with her. There chanced to be in the gathering a small detachment of soldiers from the castle garrison who had come there through pure curiosity. Near the close of the apparition, as Bernadette rose to advance towards the bush, thereby drawing closer to the lady, two of these soldiers offered their services in order to facilitate her movements. "Come now,—room, room, here!" cried the two as they walked backwards, and pushed the crowds from right to left, as if they were obeying a command. "And to think," said one to the other, "that people will tell you and me that the apparition is an illusion! Ah! but wait,—it is with me that these cheap fellow-soldiers will have to deal!" True it was that it sufficed to see in order to believe, and that the most obstinate scepticism had to give way before such evidence. For the last time Bernadette made a deep reverence, and, the lady having disappeared, she went to church to attend Mass in company with her aunt. A great many people followed them.

To-day's apparition, as we have said, consisted solely in personal and intimate communications which Bernadette has never revealed. And such was the apparition on the following day.

The Blessed Virgin was solicitous about the spiritual development of the child she had chosen for her messenger, and by that means she wishes us to understand that the perfection of our lives is first and foremost,— a most indispensable task.

Nevertheless, the interview that followed was marked by an incident which might be of interest,— for everything in this marvelous story, even to the smallest detail, contains for each one of us, the most useful lessons. A pious lady of Lourdes (Pauline Sens, dressmaker) had given her rosary to Bernadette, asking the child to use it in presence of the apparition, and then to return it to her in order that the same rosary, consecrated by the gaze of the Virgin, might be kept as a precious souvenir of her. Bernadette, seeing no objection, naturally consented; and she thereupon began the recitation with this rosary in hand. The Celestial Lady assumed a serious aspect and said to her: "Where is your own rosary?" Bernadette lifted the one she held in hand; "You are mistaken," replied the lady, "that rosary is not yours." Thereupon the child drew her own from her pocket, and showed it to her. Instantly, the features of the Heavenly Teacher resumed their kindly expression, and the prayer of the docile child continued in all its accustomed fervor. At the sight of Bernadette's actions, all those present who carried beads, and they were in the majority, imitated her in elevating in her presence and with indescribable enthusiasm, this wonderful instrument of piety. In so doing, they actually believed they were responding to an invitation from Mary,—happy at the thought that they were attracting upon themselves her benevolent gaze. They soon learned from Bernadette what had really taken place between the lady and herself.

In asking the child to show her rosary, the Blessed Virgin wished, first of all, to inculcate in our hearts the importance which she attaches to this pious object, and the desire she has that we should all possess a rosary, our own rosary, and that we should carry it on our person in order to recite it each day.   In the second place, a reproach accompanied this question; and why? Because Bernadette made use of a rosary which was not hers; for, at the time of the apparition, the decree of Pope Alexander VII (February 6, 1657) was still in force.   In virtue of this act the indulgences attached to the use of objects of piety,—as for instance the rosary, could be gained only by persons in whose behalf these objects were indulgenced.   As a result one did not gain the indulgences if he used another's rosary. The new code of Canon Law (Article 924) has abrogated this decree; consequently, the indulgences of the rosary, instead of being, as formerly, attached to the person, are now linked to the object itself, and follow it, irrespective of the person using it (except in the case of a sale).

Here again the Blessed Virgin teaches us a twofold lesson: First—In drawing our attention to the importance of indulgences, which constitute favors so precious that in order to gain them we should use extreme care in the exact observance of conditions imposed.   Second—In teaching us the respect we should have for all the ordinances of Holy Church which has received from our Lord Jesus Christ the power to regulate all that in any way concerns divine worship.

What a precious memorial for the happy witnesses of the rosary scene which we have just described,—for having been able to produce their own rosaries before the divine Mary and recite them under her eyes! But every time that we pay her this homage,—the recitation of the rosary, do we suppose that Mary ignores us, that she does not heed our prayers? Pilgrims of desire, let us each day go in spirit before the blessed rock where eighteen times she appeared with the rosary, and where she taught Bernadette to recite it piously. Let us use it before her as did the child. Saint Francis de Sales used to say that all the gold in this world would not buy one "Hail Mary" devoutly recited. Indeed, what fortune would bear comparison with the maternal expression with which Mary answers our salutations!

INVOCATION

Hail, Mary.

"O Mary, Queen of the holy rosary, in appearing at Lourdes with a rosary, thou didst wish to remind us of this wonderful devotion, to the recitation of which thou hast at all times attached so many precious favors. Since this homage is pleasing to thy heart, we promise to be more and more faithful to it,—and every day we will offer thee this crown of *Aves*,—crown so glorious to thee, and so profitable and salutary to us.

"Our Lady of Lourdes, pray for us."

CHAPTER XIII

FOURTEENTH APPARITION

"I want people to come here in procession"

Two apparitions had already taken place since Bernadette, through obedience to the lady of the Grotto, had visited the Pastor of Lourdes. You recall from our description of the interview, the worthy Pastor's answer to the message transmitted to him by the child relative to the erection of a chapel. The Curé requested that the name of the mysterious lady be given to him, together with conclusive proofs. No doubt, this interview, characterized as it was by a feeling of distrust on the part of the Pastor, was reported faithfully to the lady by the visionary. The people commented upon it as somewhat exaggerated. After so many miracles, of which the constantly increasing importance of the pilgrimage is not the least noteworthy, we are possibly inclined to judge in like fashion. This would be a mistake; for all the superabundant proofs that we possess to-day were lacking to the Curé of Lourdes. The whole affair was still in its infancy, and he was a man of too broad experience not to mistrust the wild enthusiasm of the multitudes. Furthermore, he felt the weight of responsibility and the great harm which might result to religion and to his flock in particular, if he acquiesced too easily in this matter. His strict reserve has benefited the works of Lourdes as well as the truth, and in consequence, we must praise his wisdom. In this particular circumstance as always, God had well chosen His representative. Just how the Curé's answer was received by the lady we do not know, for the child has never revealed it.

In the course of the meeting, Tuesday, March 9, a new step will be taken towards the eventual solution. Bernadette, whom her Aunt Basile had accompanied to the Grotto, conversed as formerly with the lady and in the same ecstatic conditions. The vision ended, she rose and retired as usual. But strangely enough her countenance assumed a rather troubled aspect; to her aunt who asked her to explain the change, she replied that the lady had given her a second message for the Reverend Pastor. Urged by the child to accompany her to the rectory, Aunt Basile reluctantly consented.

For the last three days the events of the Grotto had made rapid strides. The stream of water at the fountain had taken on increased proportions, and many a miracle had testified to Bernadette's sincerity. There was certainly matter enough to alter the unfavorable disposition of the stern Pastor. In the face of a well-authenticated miracle, common sense and good faith must acquiesce and all objections vanish. In fact Abbé Peyramale had neither seen nor controlled anything himself personally. True to his line of conduct he refrained, therefore, from intervening directly; what knowledge he possessed was the result of hearsay.   He was still only on the road to conversion.

Most naturally, therefore, it was with a cold reserve that he received Bernadette.   "Well," said he to the child, "what news have you?   Has the lady spoken to you?"

"Yes, M. le Curé; she wished me to tell you once more that she desires that a chapel be erected at Massabielle;" furthermore, she added: 'I want people to come here in procession.' "

At these words, the Curé's features took on a gloomy aspect.   Harshly he replied: "My daughter, evidently this new affair was the only thing lacking to complete your string of stories; either you are lying, or the lady who speaks to you is playing the part of the one she wishes to imitate.   She insists upon processions, and why?   No doubt to provoke mockery on the part of the unbeliever, and thereby to discredit religion.   The trap isn't an intelligent one.   Tell her in my behalf, that she does not well understand the attributions of the clergy; if she were really the lady she represents, she would know that I haven't the right to take the initiative in a similar manifestation; you should have been sent to the Bishop of Tarbes and not to me."

"But, M. le Curé," interrupted Bernadette, rather timidly, "the lady did not tell me that she wanted a procession to the Grotto at the present time,—she simply said: 'I want people to come here in procession;'

and, if I am not mistaken, she had reference to the future and not to the present time."

This remark, uttered so naturally by Bernadette, aroused the good Curé's suspicion. 'Tis a clever means, thought he, of extricating herself from a real embarrassment; the distinction was too subtle not to arouse serious doubts in his mind. Or again, this child in her simplicity was perhaps acting a part that had been taught her. Yes, certainly, the answer was a clever one. But who will fail to perceive in this, as well as in all other similar circumstances in which Bernadette has already found or will find herself in the future, the assistance promised by our Lord to His witnesses: "When they shall bring you into the synagogues, and to magistrates and powers, be not solicitous how or what you shall answer, or what you shall say; for the Holy Ghost shall teach you in the same hour what you must say." (Luke xii, 11-12.) Chafing under a sense of distrust, the Curé, after a moment of silence, said to Bernadette: "Let us see! It is time that all this should end; you tell this lady that, with the Pastor of Lourdes, one must be precise and to the point. She wants a chapel; she wants processions; under what title does she claim these honors? Who is she? Whence does she come? Let us speak plainly; I will suggest a means of making herself known:—she appears at the Grotto, just over a rosebush,—did you not say? Very well! then ask her on my part that, some day, in the presence of the multitude, she command the entire

HIS LORDSHIP
BISHOP SCHOEPFER OF TARBES
AND LOURDES

HIS LORDSHIP
BISHOP LAURENCE OF TARBES
At the time of the apparitions

GROUP OF FRIENDS AND RELATIVES
Arrow points at Bernadette. On the extreme right is her mother.

rosebush to blossom; when you announce to me that this prodigy has been actually accomplished, I will believe you, and I will accompany you to Massabielle!" Both Bernadette and her aunt smiled graciously; and having saluted M. le Curé, they departed.

The excellent Pastor wanted miracles,—he was right and he will get them; but it wasn't of his province to designate them; God receives directions from no one, neither as to time nor kind. The Pastor of Lourdes, as a matter of duty, did not fail to acquaint his Bishop with these new events in his parish; and, following his second interview with Bernadette, he went to Tarbes, there to confer with the venerable head of the diocese. The prelate, whose name was Bishop Laurence, enjoyed throughout the country, but more particularly in his own diocese, a reputation of wisdom, learning, and straightforwardness. He was an administrator of high merit, a Pastor endowed with the most eminent virtues. As in the case of Abbé Peyramale, he was truly, in the present circumstances, the man of Divine Providence. Wiser than St. Thomas he refrained from denying, he waited,—he waited a long time. In his interviews with the Curé of Lourdes he devised the most practical means of acquainting himself each day with the events,—either at Massabielle or elsewhere, pertaining to the apparitions; and the strict reserve which he himself adopted, was prescribed to his entire clergy.

INVOCATION

Hail, Mary.

"O Mary, Queen and Mother, thou hast deigned to establish at Lourdes a new throne of power and kindness, and thou invitest there thy children. It is with heart and soul that, as pilgrims of desire, we join the vast concourse of people who constantly replace one another at Lourdes, to praise thy greatness and thank thee for thy favors.

"Our Lady of Lourdes, pray for us."

CHAPTER XIV

SECOND DECEPTION

The Press and the Civil Authorities—The Soubirous

BERNADETTE, after her second visit to the rectory, had lost neither courage nor confidence; still she was much saddened and she longed for the morrow, hoping to find at the feet of her Heavenly Friend the consolation of which she felt so much need. What cared she for the approbation of the multitude? It was the Pastor's that she craved, and she had received from him but cruel rebuffs. In the anxiety of her heart, she wondered if she herself had not been the cause of the failure of her mission.

The following morning she hastened to the Grotto. And how she longed to reach it! After kneeling at her accustomed place she kissed the earth as she had often done before, ever since the Blessed Virgin had taught her this act of humility. Then, having made the sign of the cross, she recited her beads,—her eyes resting on the spot directly over the rosebush; but only the cold, bleak rock responded to her gaze. After a long wait, she stooped, kissed the earth once more and then calm and resigned, she departed,—putting in practice no doubt, for the days of adversity, the counsels that she had received in her previous meetings. "The lady has not come," said she sorrowfully to those who questioned her. "The apparitions, possibly, have come to an end," cried another voice. "I do not know," replied the visionary; "at all events, I shall return to-morrow."

In fact, the following day was the last of the fortnight requested,—and promised. As all supposed that it would mark the end of the apparitions, an extraordinary multitude invaded the little city during the entire day. From every highway great throngs kept pouring in,—on foot, on horseback, in vehicles of all descriptions, from the rustic-seated cart to the most sumptuous equipages. All the hotels and principal dwellings were taxed to their capacity; many were compelled to spend the night in the open. Even after sunset, the arrival of visitors continued; for the most part they hailed from southern France and northern Spain.

It is useless to dwell upon the fame that the events at Lourdes had already acquired. Public opinion was filled with it almost to a state of frenzy. All the French publications as well as those from outside gave it ample space, and sharp controversies ensued. It is the impious sheet that created the most turmoil. What! Apparitions, ecstasies, miracles! Come! Come! Is it possible? Science had so well proved that such things do not exist, but are, rather, the product of wild imagination or clerical invention. And to-day, this idea of the supernatural, so triumphantly denied, became so manifest that nobody could question it.

What a terrible defeat and loss of prestige, unless this idea were annihilated without delay,—unless this popular enthusiasm which had reached alarming proportions, were smothered! As might be expected, yellow journalism resorted to its customary means:—jest, falsehood, calumny; it is never a question of authenticated miracles, but the most ridiculous, the most childish stories are invented as a means of discrediting the real facts.

Vain efforts,—which after all resulted in giving the events at Lourdes a tremendous amount of publicity. Eventually, experience will teach this shameful and disloyal press a more tactful means,—the conspiracy of silence. Alone, "Le Lavedan," a small free-thinking sheet of Lourdes, situated in the midst of all these events,—unable therefore to deny them, had already adopted this cowardly and dishonest method of ignoring them. "One would have thought," said a contemporary writer, "that this paper was edited in some remote corner of the globe." As far as the civil authorities of the city, county, and capital were concerned, they stood in absolute bewilderment. We have already spoken of the attempts made to prevent Bernadette from returning to the Grotto; whilst waiting for new measures, they had become overwhelmed.

They now resorted to ruse; traps of all kinds were laid for Bernadette and her family in order to catch them in some offense or irregularity which would serve as a pretext for dragging them before the courts.

As a means of tempting this poor family offers of money were used as a bait; oftentimes the visitors, some inspired by a sense of pity or tenderness of heart, but others animated by entirely different motives, offered the Soubirous material aid,—provisions and money. But the child and her parents invariably refused all help, and in such a manner as to preclude the slightest insistence. . . . One evening a stranger calls at the lowly homestead; he questions Bernadette most minutely, congratulates her upon her happiness, and, filled with pity at the sight of such poverty, he tells her: "I am wealthy,—allow me to assist you;" and he deposits a purse of gold upon the table. Bernadette, blushing with indignation, replied vehemently: "I wish for nothing, sir,—take that away." "But it is not for you my child,—it is for your parents who appear so much in need." "We wish for nothing," retorted Bernadette's parents, "take away your gold." The stranger visibly disconcerted, picked up his purse and departed; such a strange attitude could only provoke suspicion. . . . Then again, a strange lady, after having conversed at length with Bernadette, kissed her and secretly slipped a roll of money in the folds of her apron. The child was seated; jumping to her feet as if a hot coal had fallen upon her, she allowed the precious parcel to roll upon the floor. Realizing, nevertheless, that she had acted rather awkwardly, she picked it up, and courteously returned it to the charitable lady who understood full well and admired her for it.

And yet, there wasn't always sufficient bread in the Soubirous home to satisfy the hunger of its eight members,—especially since the present events hampered the father's occupation and rendered almost useless that of his wife's; for the little home was never without visitors, eager to see and question. Mr. Estrade and Dr. Dozous, in their writings, paid homage to such noble and worthy distinterestedness; for it contributed in no small degree to enhance the esteem of these wonderful people and to strengthen the confidence in the sincerity of their child. The Soubirous, imbued with this delicate sense of privileged souls, understood full well that by accepting the smallest gift they would give the impression of commercializing things divine. What a lesson for an age where people trample under foot their most sacred obligations and sell for a little coin their honor, their conscience, and their faith!

INVOCATION

Hail, Mary.

"O Mother of Good Counsel, during thy mortal life, thou didst despise all worldly things,—because in thy wisdom, thou didst understand how vile they are in comparison with divine possessions. As thou didst for Bernadette and her God-fearing family, fill our hearts with the same sentiment, which, after all, is heavenly, and which inspired these words of St. Ignatius: 'How little the world appeals to me when I lift my eyes heavenward!'

"Our Lady of Lourdes, pray for us."

CHAPTER XV

FIFTEENTH APPARITION

Last Day of the "Fortnight"—The Multitude
Enthusiasm

THE long awaited day of days has begun to break and
already very little space at the Grotto is available;
every inch of ground seems occupied;—along the cliffs,
on both banks of the Gave, in the fields beyond, perched
in the trees, in the crevices of the rocks, in every conceivable nook, and as far as the eye can see,—it is one
solid mass of humanity. And yet, perfect order pre-
vails; apparently all seemed to realize that they were
treading on sacred soil, as on the pavement of a temple.
"The number of spectators," writes Mr. Estrade, "was
estimated at from fifteen to twenty thousand." In
anticipation of this gathering, the mayor of Lourdes
had taken precautionary measures; he arranged to have
three brigades of soldiery brought from the nearest
barracks, and requisitioned, for the maintenance of
good order, all the men at the fortress who were off
duty. At dawn, the soldiers, in dress uniform and with
drawn bayonets were stationed along the route Bernadette was to follow. The gendarmes, some on foot,
others on horseback, kept the people moving on the
streets. The local brigade acting as a picket of honor
occupied a position under the arcade of the Grotto. In

the distance, lining the banks of the Gave, could be seen the gilded helmets of a troop of cavalry sent from the neighboring city of Tarbes. There, also, stood the mayor and his council, the procurator, and the commissary, all girdled with their respective scarfs. No doubt their presence could not be construed as an expression of good will; yet they were bound to respect the rules of propriety.

One would have imagined, from all this solemn preparation, that a great personage, an illustrious princess was expected. It was better than that; it was a princess from Heaven who was about to descend upon earth, and confer with a friend, also a princess of royal poverty. And thus, everything seemed to contribute, even on the part of the adversaries, to give the close of the "fortnight" a most unexpected solemnity.

Soon the sun, whose appearance is always tardy in the valley, springs from behind the summit of the "Grand-Jer," its rays add a brilliant hue to the multi-colored costumes and head-dress,—a spectacle new to the Gave, but henceforth, to be reproduced indefinitely.

Everybody is in expectation when, suddenly, the cry: "Here she comes!" flying from mouth to mouth, sends through the vast assembly a thrill of respect. Heads are bared, hands are joined in prayer, and all eyes are focussed upon the spot whence the visionary is to appear. Bernadette advances in company with her mother,—both vested in their modest Sunday garments and wearing white hoods. They are preceded by two gendarmes who, with drawn swords, open up a lane for the two women. Neither this solemn setting nor the vast multitude which really worships her and bows respectfully as she passes seem to trouble the young girl; she appears so indifferent that one would imagine that she does not see them; her heart was there long before the people, and her mind is entirely pre-occupied with the cherished visit of the one she loves. And yet, withal, she stops suddenly; on the edge of the lane she is following, a blind girl stands there, weeping aloud; Bernadette sees her and, filled with emotion, she grasps her hands and kisses her most tenderly. She then passes on to the Grotto.

It was 7:15 A. M. when she reached her chosen spot. Kneeling without delay, she made the sign of the cross with fervor and dignity and started the recitation of the beads. After a few moments the vision began; it was noticeable to the spectators through the transformation and the brilliancy of the visionary's countenance. A profound silence spread over the entire gathering,—for the scene was a celestial one and never to be forgotten. Bernadette prayed and all prayed with her; in turn, she spoke and listened, but no one could grasp the ineffable conversation. At a certain moment, her features became saddened, and tears rolled down her cheeks; however, this was of short duration and her countenance became radiant once more. After an hour of ecstasy, the transfigured

ONE OF LOURDES' GREAT THRONGS

body resumed its natural aspect,—the vision had come to an end.

The visionary, having once more returned to her poor humble self, rose in silence and resumed her journey homeward. The gendarmes, themselves overcome with emotion, returned to their posts directly ahead of her; but this time, it was less a police escort than an escort of honor. As she advanced, her ears must have been deafened by the acclamations of the people; everybody wanted to see and touch her,—and the soldiers were compelled to act quickly in order to protect her from the excited multitudes. On the outskirts of the city this protection became altogether inadequate; a group of women broke through the lines, seized Bernadette, and showered kisses upon her. It was marvelous to witness this humble child in the midst of such a stupendous ovation, apparently unconcerned, and in full possession of her amiable simplicity; she realized full well to whom these homages belonged. One felt that her heart was still under the influence of the august presence of her Celestial Visitor. What cared this heavenly soul for worldly honors! Pride found but little favor with the Virgin's humble pupil. In this interview, Bernadette received no new message nor communications; what took place between the Heavenly Queen and her little friend has always remained a secret.

The immense throng, in its enthusiasm, was nevertheless somewhat disconcerted. A direct manifestation of the lady had been eagerly expected; her name was still an enigma,—although every one surmised that it was the Mother of Christ. And the miracle requested by the Curé of Lourdes, that is, the blossoming of the rosebush, had not occurred. The "fortnight" was over, but the solution was yet to come; everybody felt this, and as a consequence all were satisfied to wait. As for Bernadette, she replied to those who questioned her that she knew nothing, but that she would continue to visit the Grotto.

INVOCATION

Hail, Mary.

"O glorious Virgin, the glory which surrounds thee is the radiation of God's own glory, to Whom all converges. In order that some day, we may partake of it in His blessed eternity, teach us, as thou didst Bernadette, the essence of humility and its practice in every circumstance as well as in every state of life.

"Our Lady of Lourdes, pray for us."

CHAPTER XVI

DIVERSE CURES

J. Bouhohorts—C. Latapie—B. Cazeaux—B. Soupenne
Peculiar Mentality of the Adversaries

BOURRIETTE's cure, which we have already described, was the first miracle confirming the supernatural character of the new fountain at the Grotto. Others followed in quick succession,—each one creating more and more amazement and resulting in unbounded enthusiasm. Unable to relate them all, the writer has selected a few for the reader's edification.

First—Sunday evening, February 28, the day of the twelfth apparition, a most heart-rending scene took place in the home of a poor laborer. A child of two years, crippled from birth and worn out by a slow, lingering fever, was at death's door. The father, calm and resigned, and the mother hysterical with grief, looked on as life was slowly ebbing away. A sympathetic neighbor was already at work preparing the linen for the baby's burial. The little one's eyes had become glassy, its limbs rigid, the pulsations of the heart almost imperceptible.

"He is dead," cried the father.

"Go and weep by the fireplace," said the neighbor to the disconsolate mother, "I will see after everything."

But the mother did not seem to understand. Suddenly seizing her child from the cradle, she wrapped it up in her apron, crying: "He is not dead,—the Virgin of the Grotto will cure him." And she dashed out of the house. "Do not hinder me," she cried, as her husband tried to intercept her, "I am running to the Virgin." And off she fled with her precious burden. It was five o'clock in the afternoon and many hundreds of persons had congregated at the Grotto. The poor woman, praying aloud, drags herself upon her knees to the edge of the fountain. Uncovering the seemingly lifeless little form she makes the sign of the cross upon it, then, without a moment's hesitation she plunges it into the icy waters up to its head.

The spectators are horrified: "She is crazy! she is going to kill her child!"

"Do not prevent me," cried the mother, "I'm doing what I can,—God and the Virgin will do the rest." After an immersion of fifteen minutes she withdrew the little body from the water;—it was as rigid as a corpse. In all haste she returned to her home and laid the little form in its cradle.

"Can you not see that he is dead?" cried the father.

"No," said she, "he is not dead, the Blessed Virgin will cure him." After a few brief moments the mother shouted: "He breathes!" It was true; the child breathed and slept peacefully, awaking the following morning perfectly rested, rosy cheeked, and a smile on his lips. Soon he cried for nourishment which he took with delight. He was cured, not only of his fever, but also of his infirmities. During the day, having been left alone for a moment, he jumped from his cradle and when his mother arrived he ran and threw himself into her arms. It was the first time that the child had ever walked. Dr. Vergez in reporting the case officially, concludes in these terms: "The mother, to obtain her child's recovery, had recourse to means condemned by experience and medical reasoning, —and still she obtained it. This cure was effected without the ordinary stages of convalescence and in a most supernatural fashion." Drs. Peyrus and Dozous reported on the case in like manner. The baby thus revived in the waters of the Grotto is named Justin Bouhohorts, now well known in Lourdes. (See Supplementary Note VI, page 200.)

Second—A woman of thirty-eight years, Catherine Latapie, of Loubajac, four and one-half miles from Lourdes, had figured in an accident in October, 1856, which deprived her of the use of her left hand. Three fingers had remained curved in such a way as to preclude all possibility of straightening them. After having vainly treated her for eighteen months her doctor finally admitted that her ailment was incurable. The wonderful happenings at Lourdes sent a ray of hope in this poor mother's heart. On March 1, 1858, she went with her children to the Grotto, now famous throughout the entire region. After a series of fervent prayers she dipped the affected hand into the miraculous fountain and instantly she felt a relief; her fingers became normal and as flexible as before the accident.

Third—Benoite Cazeaux, of Lourdes, had been confined to her bed for three years with a lingering fever accompanied by excruciating pains in her side. The most renowned physicians had brought her no relief; she had even tried without result the sulphurous waters of Gazost. Finally, having requested that water be brought to her from the Grotto, she drank of it, bathed the affected parts of her body with it, and the disease left her instantly.

Fourth—A lady fifty years of age, Blaisette Soupenne, was afflicted with a chronic disease of the eyes which caused her much suffering; a multitude of tiny flesh growths covered her eyelids which were turned inside out. Here again medical science had exhausted all its resources; the popular waters of Gazost, Barèges, and Cauterets were all tried in turn but to no avail. The first time she made use of the miraculous water at the Grotto she experienced a notable relief. The following day she applied the same lotion, this time with absolute success. The growths disappeared, the eyes and eyelids resumed their normal aspect, and perfect vision was once more restored.

All these happy people, cured by their faith in the water of the Grotto, lived at Lourdes or in the neighborhood. Their number might have been considerably augmented by gathering from the adjoining hamlets marvels of a similar nature,—all due to the maternal care of Mary. Each day brought to Lourdes, from far and wide, persons who had benefited by the Virgin's intercession, coming with friends and relatives to thank their Heavenly Queen for favors received.

The cures which we have just related offer irrefutable testimony in favor of the supernatural events of the Grotto. To doubt had presently become an impossibility for all these fortunate ones were known throughout the entire city, so it became easy to ascertain the real facts. One could consult the physicians who treated them or examine the certified accounts of the cures which these practitioners never hesitated to furnish, and in most cases all such testimonies were accompanied by an act of faith in the intervention of a supernatural power. It was science pure and simple which, either willingly or under the pressure of evidence, proclaimed the existence of the miracle. But the power of newly inculcated ideas and prejudice is enormous with certain classes who pose as learned and well-informed. For these poor people there is an axiom which says that miracles do not, and, as a matter of fact, cannot exist; and why? They are unable to answer; a moment's reflection would clearly show them that, to deny God the power of performing miracles, would be to deny His very existence;—for one cannot conceive of a God who is not allpowerful, of a God limited in some of His attributes; with God, it is everything or nothing. In such a state of mind common sense is out of question. Furthermore, how can they pretend to be in good faith? When everybody proclaims a miracle, how easy it is to go and satisfy one's self, to verify the facts, to study and analyze them, in order to ascertain whether there is truth or falsehood! And what happens? This simple procedure is overlooked, is purposely cast aside by the enemies of the supernatural, and they continue to deny,—having seen nothing, because they deliberately remain blindfolded. Such an attitude, applied to the ordinary things of life, would warrant them the surname of "Fools." In the present case it reveals but one thing, the fear of being compelled to admit facts that would hurt their pride; and, apart from being inconsistent, they would dread the loss of prestige and the necessity of sacrificing beyond measure. Such a conduct is certainly most disloyal; yet it was the attitude adopted by the officials, both at Lourdes and in the provinces; we will soon witness their guilty excesses. The people with their common sense and loyalty reasoned much differently; in the presence of the many wonders which appeared before their eyes, they allowed themselves to be guided by faith in, and by gratitude toward, God and the august distributor of His mercies.

INVOCATION

Hail, Mary.

"O thou whom the Church, having long benefited by thy power and kindness, tells us to invoke under the title of 'Health of the Sick,' look down graciously upon our poor invalids, and in thy wisdom, obtain for them the most advantageous grace for the salvation of their souls:—their recovery, or at least the alleviation of their sufferings, but more especially a real Christian resignation which brings to the afflicted so great a reward.

"Our Lady of Lourdes, pray for us."

CHAPTER XVII

AFTER THE "FORTNIGHT"—BERNADETTE
At School—At the Grotto

FROM the outset of the apparitions, Lourdes and the entire Pyrenean region had been blessed with exceptionally fine weather. It was truly a premature spring, as winter in obedience to the Creator's command had suspended its rigors. This unusual occurrence contributed no little to attract the multitudes to Massabielle. But behold! after an eventful fortnight, weather conditions became suddenly changed; spring receded temporarily and winter came back to its own. On March fifth, and the following day, snow fell in abundance and the thermometer dropped considerably. The rush to the Grotto, where no more apparitions were expected, naturally subsided.

As to Bernadette, her life as a scholar was rendered more peaceful and more natural,—for the number of visitors gradually diminished. Every morning, after having helped her mother at home, (being the oldest of the family) she would start for school, her lunch basket upon her arm. No one, as she strolled along, would have imagined that she was the heroine of the marvelous events which for three weeks had caused so much sensation at home and abroad. Nothing distinguished her from the rest of the children,—she was attired as the little girls of the poor class. Towards all without distinction, she was good-natured, unaffected, kind and gentle, willingly joining them at play. It was remarked that in her conversations she never made the slightest allusion to the apparitions of the Grotto, referring to them simply when questioned, —modesty and patience characterizing her answers. Whenever her attention was called to the apparitions one felt that she was about to perform a sort of ministry,—that of serving in the capacity of witness to the Heavenly Lady. Nothing affected her patience, neither the idle or captious questions nor the prolonged interviews from which she frequently emerged in a state of weakness and fatigue. She never manifested the slightest displeasure; but she often admitted that all such visits caused her to fear. She possessed the rare virtue of overcoming this repugnance and always appeared most amiable to her visitors.

In school, as well as in her catechism classes, she maintained the same modest attitude, shunning all publicity, and applying herself with very slow progress to the study of the alphabet and religious doctrine. She was a most tractable child.

First communion was the culmination of all her desires and she prepared for it with every effort of her mind and soul. Her piety, devoid of ostentation, was profound and most sincere; when she prayed it was from her whole heart. There was nothing studied in her, everything was most natural;—her attitude, her bearing, her language. As is commonly found with children she was concerned only with the present,—the past and future troubled her but little, as if nothing extraordinary had crossed her path. Was not this demeanor the result of lessons received at the Grotto,— lessons of humility, modesty, abnegation, and charity? And yet, in the hidden sanctuary of her soul, the place of honor was reserved for the Heavenly Lady with whom her mind and her heart were irrevocably linked. Her life was brightened by the memory of that happiness she had fifteen times enjoyed. Her memory, rebellious as a rule, proved most faithful when dealing with the apparitions. How well she would recall the minutest details of each of them,—even repeating to herself every syllable which had fallen from the Virgin's lips. She continued to be within herself the happy visionary of the Grotto. And such were her school days,—simple, innocent, and well occupied, as were those of her companions.

After school hours, she would run alone to her cherished Grotto. Wearing her customary head-dress she would pass unnoticed among the many groups who strolled back and forth,—for the Grotto was never empty. At all hours of the day people could be seen kneeling in prayerful attitude. Popular devotion had transformed Massabielle into a veritable chapel:—in the background, a rustic altar, surmounted by a statue of the Virgin, was banked with flowers and with a variety of religious objects. Numerous candles burned uninterruptedly. Hundreds of visitors, beads in hand, prayed as never before. At times these prayers took the form of hymns and canticles. It was the Queen of Heaven they invoked under her most pleasing titles: —Immaculate Virgin, Mother of Mercy, Refuge of Sinners, Help of the Sick, Gate of Heaven, Help of Christians. The most popular hymns to Mary alternated between the "Ave Maris Stella" and the "Magnificat."

Arriving at the Grotto, Bernadette would kneel near the fountain, which she was instrumental in creating, and drink of its miraculous water. Then in order to avoid attention, she would cross the spot occupied by her during the apparitions and seek refuge in some obscure corner of the Grotto. There, after kneeling, she would kiss the earth, make the sign of the cross, and devoutly recite her rosary,—her eyes in the meantime resting upon the spot where her Celestial Friend had appeared to her. As evening drew near she would kiss the earth once more, bow respectfully to the statue upon the altar and resume her journey homeward. On the way, in imitation of Mary of Nazareth, she reviewed the many marvels of which she had been, at the Grotto, the humble intermediary. On holidays, as the pious child enjoyed more time to herself, she would spend long hours at the Grotto in company with the wonderful lady who had promised to make her happy, —*not in this world but in the next*. But did she not in reality enjoy true happiness, at least during these too short moments?

INVOCATION

Hail, Mary.

"O most amiable Virgin, Bernadette has seen thee, and from that moment her soul is filled with thee,—Heaven is in her heart. What delights must God prepare for those who will see Him in person, in all His glory, in the midst of the Celestial Court! May this ray of Heaven, with which thou hast illumined the Grotto of Lourdes, remain in our minds, to enlighten, console and encourage us.

"Our Lady of Lourdes, pray for us."

CHAPTER XVIII

THE QUARRYMEN AT THE GROTTO

A New Road—The Truce of the Criminals

PILGRIMAGES to the Grotto of Massabielle were definitely established; no power on earth will henceforth suppress or diminish them; earth has answered the appeal of Heaven.

The marvelous events which we have related have created this religious enthusiasm of the people, without the coöperation of ecclesiastical influence:—"*A Domino factum est istud*, (It is the direct work of God.)" Massabielle, which only yesterday was nothing but an unknown wilderness, had acquired over night a power of attraction that increased day by day. The miracles which were being multiplied had appealed to popular devotion and consecrated the place as a most venerated shrine. Rich and poor, learned and ignorant, men, women, and children,—all without distinction visited the Grotto in ever increasing numbers.

We have already stated that following Bourriette's miraculous recovery the corporation of quarrymen, of which he was a member, expressed their gratitude to the august Benefactress in opening a new path on the slope of the cliff as a means of facilitating the approach to the Grotto and the miraculous fountain. And their efforts did not end here.

THE SANCTUARY OF LOURDES IN THE PYRENEES

Owing to the increasing number of pilgrims, this new path soon became inadequate, so the quarrymen decided to replace it by a broad and practicable roadway.

"This," says Mr. Lasserre, in his most touching narrative, "was no mean undertaking; it required time, patience, and resources." These good men performed their task in the evening at the close of the regular daily occupation. They would seek rest after a hard day's work in opening this road that "led to God." *"In labore requies."* At nightfall one could see them as a swarm of ants on the mountain slope, digging, blasting, and carting away in wheelbarrows loads of earth, marble, and granite. "Who will pay you?" they were often asked. "The Blessed Virgin," was their answer. Before returning to their homes they would descend to the Grotto and recite the evening prayer in common. In the midst of nature's wonders, under the starry canopy of Heaven, such Christian scenes savored of a primitive simplicity and grandeur. These good laborers, all endowed with grateful hearts, gave all that was in them,—the work of their limbs and bodies.

But there were others also who expressed to the Blessed Virgin their gratitude and their love; votive offerings of all descriptions,—some quite modest, others of greater value, had accumulated on the altar steps and on the ground near-by. In order to protect them against the pressure of the multitudes, the men had surrounded them with a rustic balustrade. Lying here and there could be seen a variety of jewelry, even gold crosses and chains.

To facilitate the erection of the chapel requested by the lady of the Grotto, gifts of money began to arrive and were thrown over the balustrade and left there under the guard of public faith. Considerable sums of money, many thousands of francs, remained day and night without any exterior protection. And such was the respect that this hitherto unknown spot inspired, such was the moral effect it produced upon the people that throughout the entire country not one malefactor could be found to commit a sacrilegious theft at the Grotto. And this is all the more astonishing because only a few months previously, in that very region many churches had been pillaged. Evidently the Virgin did not wish that the smallest criminal act be linked with the origin of the pilgrimage she had come to establish.

Let us take particular notice of a most peculiar circumstance which historians have not failed to mention. It consisted in a sort of immunity which benefited the entire region for the six months that marked the period of the apparitions. During this lapse of time not one crime was committed, not one criminal was condemned; in this fact lay the immunity. This is without doubt a most unusual occurrence in the annals of France.

This strange coincidence, this mysterious indication of a hidden power which permeated the entire country, this moral prodigy seems to have been intended as a subject of meditation for the most frivolous minds.

How comes it, that during this prolonged period, the hand of the criminal has been stayed? Is it imposture, hallucination, or catalepsy? Whence came this peace, this extraordinary truce, precisely at this particular moment? Outside of the explanation we have ventured, we invite the army of unbelievers to produce a motive for this undeniable fact, for this strange coincidence. They will labor in vain. The Queen of Heaven had visited the country, she had showered her blessings as she passed.

INVOCATION

Hail, Mary.

"O Queen of Heaven, thou whose power is exercised with kindness and clemency, we thank and bless thee. Who has ever had recourse to thee, and has not felt the effects of thy bounties? We fly to thy maternal protection, as a means of precaution against the perils which threaten us.

"Our Lady of Lourdes, pray for us."

CHAPTER XIX

SIXTEENTH APPARITION

"I am the Immaculate Conception"—Universal Joy

ONE remembers that at the third apparition Bernadette had asked the lady her name, and that for sole answer she had received but a smile. Many times since then, especially after her interviews with the Pastor of Lourdes, she had vainly repeated the same question. But precisely because of the lady's silence on this point, —a most essential one, the multitude figured that she would appear again to crown the work she had undertaken. This was also Bernadette's fond hope because at the last apparition of March 4, her amiable visitor had departed without even a "farewell."

During the evening of March 24, she felt within her heart the sweet presentiment that the following day her hopes would be realized. It was more than a presentiment,—it was a positive certainty. And so before retiring she disclosed her feelings to her good parents. And why the next day? Because on March 25, the Church celebrated one of the most glorious feasts of the Blessed Virgin, the Annunciation, so dear to Christian piety,—the feast of the "Ave Maria," Heaven's salutation, brought by the Archangel Gabriel to the Virgin of Nazareth, and which Bernadette had repeated so many times under the very eyes of the Celestial Apparition.

The joy that filled her heart kept her awake during the entire night,—night of prayer and delicious expectation. At early dawn she was up. After dressing hastily, her heart bounding with joy, she was soon on her way to the Grotto. The weather once more had become beautiful and nature had resumed all her charms. The mountain peaks, crowned with an immaculate snow, sparkled with the first rays of the rising sun as Bernadette arrived at Massabielle.

Many people had preceded her. Among these could be seen some who had been the happy recipients of miraculous favors: Louis Bourriette, Blaisette Soupenne, Benoite Cazeaux, and others. Different groups from both the city and the adjoining country followed one another in rapid succession and swelled the multitude at the Grotto. All these pilgrims had been brought together by a sentiment of piety on the occasion of the feast, and to this sentiment was added a cherished hope that something new would characterize the morning of the Annunciation.

Imagine Bernadette's surprise, when on arriving, she beheld the Grotto already illumined by the celestial brilliancy of the apparition. "Calmly and with a smile on her lips," relates Bernadette, "the lady gazed at the multitude, as an affectionate mother gazes at her children." All confused, the child drops upon her knees and begs pardon for her late arrival. But let Bernadette herself describe this wonderful scene as she did to Mr. Estrade, the evening of the memorable day:—

"Always kind to me," said the child, "she signified with a movement of her head, that there was no need of my excusing myself. I then expressed to her all my affections, all my respects, and the happiness that I experienced at seeing her once more, and having opened my heart to her, I began the recitation of the rosary. In the meantime, the idea of asking her name flashed across my mind, and in such a persistent manner as to obliterate all my other thoughts. I feared lest I become annoying, in reiterating a question which had always remained unanswered; and yet, something seemed to compel me to talk. Giving way to an irresistible impulse, the words slipped from my mouth: 'Madam, will you kindly tell me your name?' In answer to this question, the lady, with a slight inclination of her head, smiled amiably but said nothing. Somewhat encouraged, notwithstanding her silence, I repeated my supplication; she renewed her smile and her gracious salutation, but remained silent. Finally, a third time, with joined hands I resumed my prayer. Presently the lady assumed a serious aspect, and appeared to humble herself; she joined both hands and placed them upon her breast, lifting at the same time her eyes heavenward; then slowly separating her hands and leaning a trifle towards me, she uttered with a trembling voice these words: 'I am the Immaculate Conception!' Immediately afterwards the august Virgin disappeared."

Bernadette emerged from this vision with a feeling of happiness more genuine, and with an exterior joy more pronounced than on all other occasions. Without being able to account for it,—(for these terms were new to her and uncomprehended) she nevertheless felt the importance of the Lady's answer which had resounded in her ears. Surrounded by the multitude and questioned relative to the interview, she repeated the words as they fell from the lips of the Celestial Lady: "I am the Immaculate Conception." These words seemed to electrify the vast assembly; they flew from mouth to mouth with acclamations of triumph and joy that reëchoed through the valley. The city was soon informed of the news and shared the enthusiasm of the pilgrims. Everywhere it was an outburst of delirious joy; no more uncertainty,—it is undeniably Mary, the Mother of God, the Queen of Heaven who has appeared at Massabielle! It was surmised at first,—now it is a matter of certainty. Hail to our Lady of Lourdes! Hail to the Immaculate Conception! This first ovation which will be followed by countless others, is beyond description; and it continued until nightfall. Throngs remained at the Grotto; everybody wanted to deposit a kiss of love and gratitude upon the rock which had been graced by the Virginal feet of the Heavenly Queen.

Bernadette left the Grotto arm in arm with her Aunt Lucille. And along the route what an ovation was accorded her!   And how she longed to break the good news to her dear parents who wept with joy,—forgetting, temporarily, all the trials and tribulations of the last six weeks,—the price they had paid for this one minute in Heaven.

The happy child lost no time in imparting the good news to the venerable Pastor.   It was eventually the answer required by the vigilant priest who received it with unutterable joy; it was for him also the realization of a secret hope.   But his mastery over himself was such that he succeeded in concealing his emotion; he still remained for a time cautious and reserved.

In the evening Bernadette paid a visit to Mlle. Estrade and to her brother, the registrar, who from the start had kept a faithful account of all these marvelous incidents that he might publish them afterwards.

"Had an angel entered my home," wrote he, "I would not have been more overjoyed.   Her description of the early morning scenes was most beautiful. Near the close of the narrative she became overwhelmed with emotion; she paused for a moment,—then, with tears in her eyes and a quiver upon her lips, she repeated, with an angelic expression, the ever memorable answer of the Virgin: 'I am the Immaculate Conception.'"

O most sublime utterance, Mary's reply to the solemn proclamation of the dogma in her honor four years previously, by Pope Pius IX!   It was also the brilliant confirmation,—accompanied by the miracle, of the entire revelation with its essential dogmas: original sin, the Incarnation, the Redemption, the establishment of the infallible Church. Glory, love, and gratitude throughout the world and unto the end of time to the Immaculate Mary, our Lady of Lourdes!

INVOCATION

Hail, Mary.

"O Virgin most pure, whom God in view of the Incarnation of the Word, has preserved from original sin, grant those who honor thy Immaculate Conception the grace of atonement for their short-comings, and that of preservation for the remainder of their lives.

"Our Lady of Lourdes, pray for us."

CHAPTER XX

CONTRADICTIONS

The Clergy—The Officials—The Freethinkers
Medical Inquiry

THERE exists a providential law, the constant application of which can be followed throughout history: no undertaking which possesses the twofold character of being at the same time human and divine can exist and prosper without suffering contradictions and persecutions. The Church of God presents the most striking example; instituted to become universal in space and time, that is, to govern the people until the end of ages, her birth and her development have been characterized by persecutions. The work of Lourdes, although inferior in scope, has not escaped this law. Having many times touched upon this question, the course of events compel us to revert to it again.

Bernadette, Mary's poor little messenger, was brought face to face with three main elements of contradiction,—all three imbued with principles of a different nature. In the first place we have the clergy. The priest, although admitting the possibility of revelation and miracles, is bound in particular cases to act cautiously and with reserve, for it is incumbent upon him to protect Christian souls against the possibility of error and superstition. But the moment that truth is proclaimed, his opposition ceases, and from adversary or prudent observer, he assumes the rôle of defender and propagator. Such was the wise attitude adopted from the start by the priests of Lourdes, as well as by those of the entire diocese,—in imitation of their Bishop.

A second category of adversaries comprises those who, placing personal interest above all else, form an opinion based upon the advantages they expect to reap. In those days, rationalism, the avowed enemy of the supernatural, was well thought of and enjoyed the favors of those in power. To this category belonged,—either through conviction or otherwise, the public officials of Lourdes and of the entire province. We have already seen them at work,—we will meet them again.

The third category is made up of those poor, unfortunate slaves of Satan, who foolishly style themselves "freethinkers". They are hopeless dissenters, avowed enemies of God and the Church, systematically closing their eyes to the truth and opposing reason with nothing but blasphemy and falsehood. They are found everywhere; bold and impudent, they cause a vast amount of turmoil, thereby creating an impression of numerical strength which in reality they do not possess. The newspaper is their medium of action, and the masonic lodges are their rally-point and inspiration. Lourdes could boast of a few of them; but the events of the Grotto kept them in a continued state of exasperation.

This digression was necessary before undertaking to relate the annoyances and persecutions to which Bernadette and the work of the Blessed Virgin at Lourdes will be subjected. Moreover, this narrative occupies too important a rank in our marvelous story to refrain from giving even a brief summary of the same. Can one fully appreciate a victory if he is not acquainted with the vicissitudes of the battle?

On the very day that the Heavenly Lady divulged to Bernadette her identity, the Curé of Lourdes lost no time in flashing the news to the Bishop of the diocese. At the same time, the mayor and the commissary instructed the head of the department, Baron Massy, prefect of the Upper Pyrenees. This high functionary was looked upon as a sincere and practical Catholic; his zeal for the interest of the Church had recently been rewarded by Pope Pius IX, who had conferred upon him the title of "Commander of the Order of St. Gregory the Great." But his religion savored of a strange inconsistency quite common among Catholics of his days and rank. He admitted the teachings of the Church relative to the supernatural, but with certain restrictions, —that is, he repudiated *a priori* all that we call divine manifestations, such as apparitions, revelations, and miracles. All such happenings excepting those that are mentioned in the Bible, were classed by him as frauds or hallucinations. As a result, he resolved to put an end to these mysterious stories of Lourdes which he believed compromising,—not so much for public order which was never violated, but rather for the honor of religion.   But why not refer the matter to the Bishop, who was certainly as interested as he was,—besides being more competent in such affairs!   Thoughtlessly, therefore, he plunged into a struggle as stupid as it was abusive, from which nevertheless, he will emerge lamentably defeated.

"If I could only have Bernadette arrested!" thought he.   But to accomplish this he had no legal pretext, since in the young girl's conduct nothing contrary to the penal code could be found; and again, it might have been dangerous in view of the over excitement of the population of Lourdes.   One practical means flashed across his mind: to obtain from a medical commission a certificate declaring the visionary insane, for by so doing, she would be interned in an asylum and all this agitation would cease.   The plan had no sooner been conceived that it was put to execution.   By an order of the prefect three physicians were appointed to examine Bernadette's mental condition.   All three were noted for their learning and honesty, but absolutely opposed to the Church and the supernatural.   Dr. Dozous, who from the start, had loyally studied Bernadette and her visions, would naturally be chosen as one of the commission; but, surmising that he believed in the apparitions, he was cleverly eliminated.   The investigation took place at the hospice where Bernadette attended class.   Simple and unaffected, ignorant of what had been planned against her, she submitted to everything, relating in detail all the apparitions and giving the required explanations. She answered frankly and with an astonishing presence of mind, all the questions both clever and insidious, that were put to her without ever being trapped or contradicting herself. The doctors, having attempted every possible ruse, were dumbfounded; they examined her in vain,—not one lesion, not one indication of an affected brain. As they had received strict orders to locate a disease of this description, and as professional honesty did not permit them to certify falsely, they drew up a report in vague and confused terms in which they arrived at no conclusions. The only satisfaction they could give the prefect was that Bernadette "might be insane." And these are the identical terms of the report. They didn't dare utter one word more.[1]

But all this did not satisfy the prefect. In vain did he search Paris for help; he sought the minister of cults, Mr. Gustave Roulaud, and requested of him a line of conduct, or rather some stringent orders behind which he could shield his own responsibilities.

Whilst waiting for a solution which was not forthcoming, the multitude at the Grotto increased each day; and to the prefect's great consternation, perfect order existed. The commissary reported that on April fifth, nine thousand pilgrims had visited the Grotto, and ten

---

[1] Dr. Balancie, of Lourdes, who drew up the report, surrendered before the irresistible eloquence of facts; and during the lapse of twenty years he signed certificates of miraculous cures wrought by the Celestial Apparition whose existence he had long denied.

thousand the following day.   And all these people did
was to pray.   But prayer, even in the open, was not as
yet classed as a legal wrong-doing against which the
powers might act.   How much more this excellent prefect would have preferred a revolt or a noisy manifestation,—either threatening public peace or not!   Let
him struggle in his agony and perplexity;—and in
spirit, let us mingle our prayers and homages with those
of the happy pilgrims of the Immaculate Virgin.

INVOCATION

Hail, Mary.

"O Virgin most wise, in allowing human contradictions to hamper
thy works at Lourdes, thou gavest us a wonderful lesson of
patience in time of trials, and of confidence in Divine help which is
always accorded good will and perseverance; grant us the grace of
keeping this precious lesson before our minds in the conduct of
our affairs, whether personal or social.

"Our Lady of Lourdes, pray for us."

CHAPTER XXI

SEVENTEENTH APPARITION

The Miracle of the Candle—The Prefect, the Mayor, the Pastor

SINCE the feast of the Annunciation, March twenty-fifth, Bernadette had not seen the Blessed Virgin. But the glorious revelation of that day was still the delight of her heart. Yes, it was the Mother of God, the Queen of Angels who appeared to her at the Grotto; she had called herself "The Immaculate Conception."

In the meantime, whilst those in power were plotting against both herself and the divine work of Lourdes, the happy child unaware of the approaching storm, pursued her quiet studies,—most attentive to the preparation of that one great affair—her first communion. Wednesday of Easter week, April seventh, she felt within her soul a secret call to the Grotto. Filled with joy she hastened to obey the familiar voice, and on her arrival she went and knelt at her chosen spot of former days, a spot which the throngs, no matter how great, had always respected. Soon the brilliancy of her countenance and her ecstatic attitude announced to the people that the Queen of Heaven had once more descended upon earth. A marvelous occurrence signalized this vision, witnessed by more than nine thousand

THE BASILICA AND THE CHURCH OF THE ROSARY

MIRACULOUS BATHS

people.   Following is Dr. Dozous' account of the phenomenon:

"Bernadette was on her knees reciting, with an angelic fervor, the prayers of her rosary which she held in her left hand, holding at the same time in her right hand a lighted candle.   Just as she began to ascend the incline on her knees as usual, something caused her to stop suddenly; at the same time, her right hand having been brought in contact with the left, placed the candle flame directly underneath the fingers of this hand,— the same being sufficiently separated one from another to allow the flame to circulate between them.   Fanned at this moment by a stiff breeze, the flame produced on her skin no alteration whatsoever.   Astounded over this strange marvel I prevented the by-standers from interfering, and, watch in hand, I was in a position to observe it perfectly for fully fifteen minutes.   Always in ecstasy, she advanced to the upper portion of the Grotto displacing her hands in the meantime and separating them,—thus removing the action of the flame.   Having finished her prayers and her transfiguration having come to an end, she rose and prepared to leave the Grotto.   I held her for a moment and begged her to show me her left hand which I examined most carefully; there wasn't the slightest trace of a burn.   Turning towards the person who had received the candle from Bernadette I asked her to light it and allow me to take it for a few moments.   I immediately placed it several times successively under the child's left hand which she withdrew, crying 'You are burning me!'"

Let us bear in mind that we have just heard a doctor of medicine, a man of science, a keen observer by profession. Was not this prodigy, which so amazed the people, a fitting answer to the medical commission which had declared timidly that Bernadette "might be insane"? And this flame which burned and melted wax, and left intact after fifteen minutes' action, Bernadette's live flesh,—could this be called hallucination? It is by means of a clear and most positive fact that the Blessed Virgin refuted, without the possibility of an argument, the "maybes" of the scientists.

A few weeks were spent in active consultation between Paris, Tarbes, and Lourdes. It was expedient that this come to an end,—for the number of pilgrims increased daily; the longer the delay the more critical the situation was bound to grow.

At the outset of the month of May, the prefect resorted to a twofold course. First, he ordered the mayor of Lourdes to seize Bernadette, and take her to "a house of rest" at Tarbes. "Her state of health," said he compassionately, "requires special treatment." Second, he enjoined the commissary to strip the Grotto of all that the piety of the people had herein deposited. The mayor had been deeply impressed by the recent events. Fearing the exasperation of the people and the ire of Heaven, accompanied by the imperial procurator, he ran to the rectory where he communicated to the Reverend Pastor the prefectoral order and begged his advice and assistance. No sooner did Abbé

Peyramale become acquainted with the proposed outrage than his indignation burst forth. Standing erect, displaying thereby his wonderful stature, with firmness in his eyes and determination in his every movement:

"Mr. Mayor," said he, "as Pastor of Lourdes, I owe myself to all without exception, but especially to the weak. The measures that you speak of are both illegal and odious; go and notify the prefect that his gendarmes will find me at this poor family's door, and that they will trample me under foot before they lay hands upon this poor little girl." Such an energetic attitude on the part of the local Pastor was more than the mayor could stand. On the same day, in a letter to the prefect, he told him frankly that there would certainly be danger of a revolt if Bernadette were molested, and that, as far as he was concerned, he absolutely refused to carry out such orders,—tendering at the same time his resignation in case he were compelled to act. And thus did Bernadette escape, unknowingly, a persecution which had been plotted against her peace and her liberty.

INVOCATION

Hail, Mary.

"O most helpful Virgin, thou who hast protected the innocence and weakness of Bernadette against the outrages of the wicked, protect us against Satan, the enemy of our souls, that we may not fall into the snares with which he hopes to drag us into an eternity of sorrow.

"Our Lady of Lourdes, pray for us."

CHAPTER XXII

THE DESPOLIATION OF THE GROTTO

The Answer of God, and That of the Public

THE wise recanting of the mayor of Lourdes whom the prefect had instructed to arrest Bernadette, was not followed by the commissary who had been ordered to despoil the Grotto. A stranger in the city, this functionary had no such motive as the mayor to respect the feelings of the people. Eager then to display his energy and his zeal, on the very day that he received the order of the prefect, May fourth, he did all in his power to comply. The religious objects and votive offerings deposited at the Grotto were so numerous that a conveyance of some sort had to be resorted to in order to carry them away. The commissary at the outset requested aid from the postmaster but he was turned down flatly; the same reception was accorded him by the liverymen. The hotel-keepers and business men alike, either through a sense of sacrilegious horror or for fear of injuring their affairs, absolutely refused to have anything to do with the outrage. Finally, after much trouble and exasperation, he succeeded in hiring a horse and team for thirty francs; "Judas's thirty pieces of coin," cried the multitude. Stung to the quick, he started for Massabielle accompanied by a number of police officers and a vast multitude of people, all calm and resigned as the atmosphere before a storm.

In a short space of time the Grotto had been stripped of everything,—flower vases, bouquets, framed pictures, statuettes, candles, and other objects. Every piece of money, whether gold, silver or copper, was carefully put aside to be turned over to the mayor. There was yet the balustrade. In order to demolish it, a hatchet was necessary; but not one laborer at a neighboring saw-mill which he visited would accommodate him. He then approached a wood chopper in the distance, who willingly acquiesced to his demand and in a short time the balustrade was reduced to kindling wood. It was a critical episode for the commissary, who performed the work personally; each stroke of the axe was answered by threatening cries on the part of the throng. Pale, distracted, and trembling with fear, the unfortunate officer had recourse to all sorts of excuses, alleging obedience to orders though much against his will. Presently,—and luckily for him, a voice was heard above all others: "Be calm,—no violence; let us leave everything in the hands of God." And only a few feet away the roaring waters of the Gave continued to roll by. This sane advice probably saved the commissary, who was enabled to leave uninjured, together with his agents and their glorious spoils. When the convoy reached the city hall the public crier visited every quarter of the city announcing that all the religious objects found at the Grotto would be returned to those who could identify them as their own. As if an order had been sent broadcast, all the women of the poorer class congregated at the municipal buildings and claimed the votive offerings that belonged to them,— even those that did not belong to them, which they returned in triumph to the Grotto. After nightfall, these same women in reparation for the outrages committed against the Blessed Virgin illumined the cliff of Massabielle with myriads of torches and candles.

The day following the odious profanation of the Grotto, news spread throughout the town that the man who had loaned his team to the commissary had two ribs fractured in an accident; and shortly afterwards, that the one who had loaned his hatchet had his two feet crushed by the fall of a plank. The population was quick to perceive in this double and unique coincidence Heaven's answer to yesterday's outrage. The people's response was correspondingly firm and energetic. Every evening, 'mid genuine enthusiasm a procession organized to the strains of the litanies started from the Old Bridge, flanked on either side by the quarrymen, and proceeded to the illuminated Grotto where all prayed long and fervently; and nobody left before drinking at the fountain. Never had a month of Mary been celebrated with so much enthusiasm and by a gathering of such proportions.

INVOCATION

Hail, Mary.

"O Mary, Help of Christians, today and more than ever, the enemies of thy divine Son would rob His good children of the faith of their Baptism; as heretofore, defend and protect the oppressed Christian souls.

"Our Lady of Lourdes, pray for us."

CHAPTER XXIII

BERNADETTE'S FIRST COMMUNION
Prayer of Mr. Henri Lasserre

THE keen struggle, the first phases of which we have just described, continued to excite the passions of the people, and Bernadette, who had been the cause of this prodigious upheaval, was completing as quietly as possible her preparation for her first communion. How her heart would have relished complete solitude in anticipation of this great event! But how could she evade the numerous visitors who wished to see her and talk of the apparitions? Sole witness of the Blessed Virgin, she felt that a sacred mission had been confided to her, and regardless of the consequences she was bound to fulfill it. Her candor, her good faith and her frankness, charmed all those with whom she came in contact.

One day a distinguished lady, inspired by a sense of real veneration, said to her: "My child, will you kindly exchange your rosary with mine?" The one she offered was made of precious stones linked together by a chain of solid gold. "Keep your rosary, madam," replied Bernadette, "mine is of an inferior quality, and is more in keeping with my condition." A visitor once offered her a bit of money, that she might have the pleasure of giving it away in charity; the young girl replied: "Give it yourself, sir, in my name,—it will mean more than if I gave it myself." Bernadette wished to serve God gratuitously, and fulfill, without forsaking her noble poverty, the mission she had received. And yet in her own home, bread was sometimes lacking.

Such exquisite delicacy, coupled with so much strength of character, clearly denoted a soul of lofty ideals and noble sentiments. But few had penetrated this wonderful sanctuary, the incomparable wealth of which no exterior sign had yet disclosed. To all strangers who did not know her,—with her simple carriage, her natural and unaffected manners, and her rustic dialect, she was in every way similar to all other little girls of her condition, possessing nothing particularly distinctive. Her character was calm and undemonstrative, her piety in like fashion. Her education was quite rudimentary, her catechism examination anything but brilliant; but who could doubt that her interior dispositions were far above the ordinary? Had she not been prepared for her first communion by the greatest and most competent teacher? In the many secret interviews which those two virginal souls had held together,—the child of the earth and the Queen of Heaven, can we not surmise that the coming meeting of Bernadette with Jesus constituted one of the principal topics of Mary's instructions to her?

It was on Thursday, June third, on the feast of the Blessed Sacrament, in the chapel of the hospice that this sublime ceremony took place. The child's piety and her recollection constituted the outstanding features. Contrary to the expectations of many, her happiness was not disclosed upon her countenance by the transfiguration produced by the vision of the Immaculate Mary at the Grotto.

That same evening, Mlle. Estrade asked her: "What made you happier,—to have received Jesus in the Holy Eucharist, or to have conversed with the Blessed Virgin at the Grotto?"

"I do not know," replied Bernadette, "those things go hand in hand, and suffer no comparisons; they are entirely different; one thing I know is, that in both instances, I was supremely happy." Oh! what a most admirable and delicious answer!

We close this chapter on Bernadette's first communion by the beautiful prayer composed by her pious historian, Mr. Henri Lasserre:

"Our Lady of Lourdes, whilst the priest taught Bernadette the catechism and the truths of the Church, it is thyself, in the silence of solitary meditation, who prepared, heart to heart, thy privileged child to receive the Sacred Body of Jesus Christ. Grant us, O Mother Divine, a similar favor, so worthy of thy tenderness for us all, and of thy love for the Divine Host Who comes to visit us. Prepare in our souls an abode as worthy of Him as it is possible for a creature to be worthy of the Creator. Grant us, O incomparable Virgin, the same sentiments that filled thy heart when, for the first time, God Incarnate visited this world, and when thou didst receive in thy womb Him Whom the Heavens cannot contain. Strengthen our faith in and our love for the Blessed Eucharist:— make us understand that, when we are weak and cowardly, there, in the Eucharist are strength and courage; when we have fallen in the mire of sin, there is purity; when we are unhappy, there is consolation; when we are poor, there is wealth; when we are slaves, there is deliverance; when we have gone astray, there is the guiding path; when we have wandered in an uncertain obscurity of the mind, there is the truth; when we are dead, there is resurrection, there is life. Teach us to love, as He deserves, this Bread of Angels, this Flesh and Blood of God. That, without this living Bread, let all be vain and insipid:—shared tendernesses, joys and pleasures, realized ambitions, conquered fortunes. That, with this Divine Bread, let all sorrows be sweetened; may everything be impregnated with its Divine savor:—hard labor, tiresome duties, injuries received, humiliations endured, and everything which may appear repugnant here on earth. O Mary, help us to love the Body of Jesus Christ, the Soul of Jesus Christ, the Divinity of Jesus Christ; help us to love the Eucharist."

INVOCATION

Hail, Mary.

"O Mary, Mother of Jesus, when we are united to Him in Holy Communion, have we not acquired a new right to call thee our Mother, and a new reason why we should receive thy maternal caresses?   We are in need of this divine nourishment for the life of our souls; make us realize the greatness of this necessity, that we may often feel the desire of receiving Him in this life, until we partake of the eternal communion in Heaven.

"Our Lady of Lourdes, pray for us."

CHAPTER XXIV

THE WATER OF THE FOUNTAIN

*Contradictory Analyses—Interdiction of the Grotto
Barricades and Arrests*

WHILE the water of the blessed fountain continued to
flow pure, abundant and salutary, the multitudes,—a
veritable human torrent, rolled their ever-increasing
waves towards the Grotto at Massabielle. The mere
thought of this prodigy created consternation in the
mind of the unfortunate prefect. And, think of it!
was he, with all his strength and skill, to see his prestige fall before the ridiculous story of a little idiot!
Profoundly humiliated in the face of his useless efforts,
he vainly sought some expedient to free himself from
a bad situation. Would he suppress the unlucky fountain that a skillfully exploited hazard had drawn from
the bosom of the earth? No, this was not to be thought
of. But how about prohibiting its use, thereby putting
an end to this epidemic of cures which fostered fanati-
cism and blind credulity in his department? All that
was necessary was to establish there, through an official
analysis, the existence of a mineral water, and consequently submitted for public use to the control of the
state.

A pharmacist by the name of Mr. Latour, from
the small village of Tire, counsellor general and a

THE BASILICA AND THE RIVER GAVE

COURT OF THE ROSARY

friend of the prefect, was immediately engaged for this work. With more courtesy than loyalty this man of learning lost no time in finding at the bottom of his retorts, elements that corresponded to the prefect's desires. With this in view, and in the most ambiguous terms, he drew up a report which ends in these words: "Without wishing to prophesy, it is safe to say, considering the general make-up and the quality of the elements which compose this water, that medical science will *probably* find therein special healing properties which will class it alongside the many waters which constitute the mineral wealth of our department." Here again we find the famous "maybe" of the medical commission, which had been ordered to find a trace of insanity in Bernadette. The pharmacist-chemist makes use of it most skillfully as he writes his prediction relative to the new fountain. But his "maybe" will enjoy no better success than that of the doctors'. His "made-to-order" analysis gave rise, as might be expected, to serious protests; distinguished chemists and professors alike contested the accuracy of his report. The entire population of Lourdes, regardless of party affiliations was roused to its highest pitch,—for all without exception, friends or enemies of the supernatural, understood the import of this serious situation. The many astounding miracles due to the waters of the Grotto were facts so clear and so consistent that not one soul dared deny them. But if science could only attribute them to certain medical qualities contained in the water, what a brilliant future for the little city which would find itself transformed into a bathing resort of the highest order! What tremendous fortune in a fountain of water whose marvelous effects would simply eclipse the slow, rare, and imperfect cures of the most renowned watering places! If, on the contrary, this water possessed absolutely no natural curative quality, then supernatural intervention would be the only explanation and Lourdes would become the rendezvous of pilgrims from every quarter of the world.

Such was the state of mind on this point throughout the entire locality, and all were of the opinion that a new official analysis was expedient. The municipal council could not treat the affair with indifference. The mayor consulted the prefect relative to the choice of a man who would produce a definite analysis of this water. At that period the most renowned chemist of southern France was Mr. Filhol, a member of the Faculty of Sciences at Toulouse. The municipal council of Lourdes, after deliberating, authorized the mayor, on June third, to confide the analysis to this eminent professor. Mr. Filhol accepted the mission,—and two months later, August seventh, he delivered his scientific report which ended as follows: "This water contains no active substance capable of giving it well-defined therapeutic properties; one can drink it with impunity." In less scientific terms it means that the water is merely ordinary drinking water free from any medical property. Science had spoken its last word, and all analyses made since then have simply confirmed Professor Filhol's.

But the prefect, in his anxiety to hasten matters, had not waited for this new turn of events. Armed with the first analysis he quickly drew up a new document headed by a preamble and despatched it to the mayor with orders to make it public after having affixed his signature. Two months later the entire document was declared worthless. Following, are the specific terms of this order:

ARTICLE 1.—It is forbidden to take water at the said fountain.

ARTICLE 2.—It is also forbidden to trespass on the city property, commonly called "Border of Massabielle."

ARTICLE 3.—A wooden fence will be erected at the entrance to the Grotto to prevent all access therein. Signboards will be erected bearing these words: "Trespassing on this property is prohibited."

ARTICLE 4.—All infractions of this order will be dealt with according to law.

The mayor submitted to the proclamation of this mandate most reluctantly and made it known to the prefect that the latter assume officially the entire responsibility of this odious act. He had become very much impressed by the ever-growing enthusiasm of the people, but especially by the marvelous cures which increased daily.

The mandate was published June eighth, and on the same day the commissary ordered the erection of fences and palisades so as to prevent, unless they were destroyed or scaled, all access to the Grotto. Guards were stationed day and night, relieving one another hourly.

Such vexatious measures savored of a provocation; cries of indignation arose from every section of the city and a revolt appeared imminent. Fortunately there were neither revolt nor disorder,—the people were content to protest by peaceful manifestations.

The Curé of Lourdes constantly admonished them against violence; as he was loved and respected by all his word was obeyed.

The infractions against the above mandate, both by the people of Lourdes and outsiders, clearly showed how childish the prefect's orders were considered. The city sergeants appointed to guard the palisades, could not begin to draw up all the required reports, nor the judges to pronounce condemnations. The longer this situation continued the more intensified it became; it meant defeat for constituted authority and a loss of prestige to the unhappy prefect.

INVOCATION

Hail, Mary.

"O Virgin most pure, the wholesome and salutary water which, through thy powerful bounty, thou hast caused to spring from the bosom of the earth, is the sweet and gracious emblem of the graces of which thou art the inexhaustible channel; may they flow in abundance upon us, that, as faithful disciples of Jesus in whom lies their source, we may possess eternal happiness in Heaven.

"Our Lady of Lourdes, pray for us."

CHAPTER XXV

EIGHTEENTH AND LAST APPARITION

Feast of Our Lady of Mt. Carmel—Distinguished Pilgrims—Emotion

WE left Bernadette on the evening of her first communion; let us return to her. What becomes of the child in the midst of all this turmoil and excitement? How she would have preferred to live in seclusion or to follow her daily routine unnoticed, in order to enjoy in the peace of her heart, her many sweet recollections! But this was not possible. Whether at home or at the hospice she was constantly harassed by visitors, and these too frequent interviews which she could not and would not avoid were followed by such physical pains as to give her parents much concern. By all means it was expedient that she be taken away from these surroundings, from Lourdes itself, in order to prevent an absolute collapse. A relative of Mr. Soubirous', who was about to leave for Cauterets, offered to take her along,—adding that she would see after all expenses. This vacation of a few weeks and the care she received in her new home gave her renewed life; for, when she returned to Lourdes, she was quite capable of resuming her ordinary occupations.

Slipping unnoticed in the midst of a throng, she would run alone to Massabielle. How well we may imagine the anguish of her heart at being unable to enter her beloved Grotto! From a distance only, and beyond the Gave, could she perceive the niche in the rock where seventeen times she had enjoyed the happiness of contemplating the Immaculate Virgin! Would she see her again? She firmly hoped so. All the recent vicissitudes at the Grotto, all the detestable quarrels could not alter her faith in the divine mission confided to her. How insignificant are the powers of this earth when compared with those from on high! She knew full well that nothing could prevent the realization of Mary's expressed wishes, and that on the spot designated a chapel would soon be erected and processions organized.

On the sixteenth of July, the feast of our Lady of Mt. Carmel, Bernadette had received Holy Communion for the fourth time. In the evening, she returned to the church to continue her morning's thanksgiving. While she prayed with her customary devotion, she heard within herself the same familiar voice calling her to Massabielle. Joyful beyond measure she leaves the church and hastens to her Aunt Basile whom she begs to accompany her. As all access to the Grotto was prohibited they followed the path that leads to the fields of La Ribère, on the right bank of the Gave directly opposite the cliff of the apparitions. A few neighbors asked them where they were going, and upon receiving an answer they followed. Little by little others fall in line until the procession attains a fairly good proportion. In the meantime a group of people praying in the fields opposite the Grotto, catch a glimpse of the child and draw closer to her. All these pious souls kneel in imitation of Bernadette and recite their beads. After a few moments the ecstatic rays illumined the visionary's countenance, and delirious with joy she cries: "Yes, yes, she is here! She bows to us and smiles from beyond the palisade." And the ecstasy began. Judging from the more brilliant and more ideally beautiful reflection which transfigured the features of the child, never did the Virgin appear more charming, never did the glory which enshrouded her seem so majestic. The colloquy was purely intimate, without the slightest exchange of words. In all the vision lasted fifteen minutes; then with a parting expression of maternal love, the Queen of Angels disappeared from the view of her little friend never to show herself to her again until they meet in the eternal vision of Heaven. And thus ended the last visit of Mary to Bernadette.

It was in the neighborhood of 8:20 in the evening. The only break in the universal silence was the rumbling of the waters of the Gave. Everything contributed to prolong the profound emotion of the faithful who had been eye-witnesses of the scene just closed. It is under this solemn impression, the memory of which will live forever, that the pious assembly dispersed, when Bernadette and her aunt returned to their homes.

But now let us go back to the left bank of the Gave, near the Grotto which had been closed to the people and which was guarded by the commissary's agents. All these obstacles, as stupid as they were illegal, far from turning visitors away appeared, on the contrary, to attract them. The bathing season was at its height. From every point of Europe, strangers, tourists, and bathers invaded the many resorts of the Pyrenees. For many months past, Lourdes had caused such a tremendous sensation throughout the world that these people took advantage of its close proximity to pay it a visit. Every day from Cauterets, Barèges, Luz, Saint-Sauveur, Eaux-Bonnes, and Bagnères-de-Bigorre, conveyances of all descriptions brought hosts of excursionists who, attracted either by curiosity or by a sense of piety, paid little heed to posted instructions or barriers. One day a stranger attempted to clear the fence:

"No trespassing here," cried the guard.

"You will find that I will pass," replied the stranger and without much concern he enters the prohibited grounds and proceeds to the Grotto.

"Your name, sir? You are under arrest."

"My name is Louis Veuillot, editor-in-chief of the 'Univers'."

At this particular epoch this name was one of the most famous of the European press, and its bearer one of the most dreaded champions of the Catholic Church. Whilst the guard was drawing up a report against the illustrious writer, a short distance away a distinguished looking lady accompanied by two young girls climbed

THE BASILICA, ESPLANADE AND GREAT CRUCIFIX

over the palisades and went and knelt at the Grotto. The three proceeded to recite the rosary aloud. At the end they stooped near the miraculous fountain and drank copiously of its water. They afterwards detached a small branch from the rosebush at the niche, bowed reverently as they made the sign of the cross, and prepared to leave. The guard was waiting for them:

"In the name of the law, I arrest you," said he; "your name, please?"

"I am Madam Admiral Bruat, Governess of His Highness, the Prince Imperial."

The poor guard was so overcome on hearing this name and title that his nervousness prevented him from writing. The noble lady smilingly inscribed upon the official's paper her own name and those of her children.

That very evening, as he read these names on the police record, the commissary trembled. The following day he informed the mayor who lost no time in consulting the prefect, and he in turn, the minister. The latter gave orders to discontinue all arrests and to annul all court proceedings.

INVOCATION

Hail, Mary.

"O Virgin most faithful, in imitation of those brave Christians who, in order to pay thee homage, pay little attention to obstacles, threats and human respect, we resolve henceforth to be more courageous in the service of Almighty God, and never to flinch in the accomplishment of our duty. Obtain for us, from thy Divine Son, the grace of remaining forever faithful to this resolution.

"Our Lady of Lourdes, pray for us."

CHAPTER XXVI
VICTORY

Intervention of the Emperor—Removal of both the Prefect and the Commissary

LONG before the stubborn opposition of the magistrates was forced to crumble, the prudent reserve of the clergy assumed a much milder character. The magnitude of the events, and the testimonies of so many trustworthy persons gradually cleared the first doubts. The Curé of Lourdes himself had not waited all this time before admitting the authenticity of the events. True to his principles, he fought with indomitable courage the development of opinions, and acquiesced only in the face of evidence. To come out openly and join the legion of pilgrims one thing alone was required, and this as a matter of discipline,—the authorization of the Ordinary; the same slow but sure transformation had been accomplished in the mind of the Bishop of Tarbes. The latter, at length realized that the time to act had come, and on the twenty-eighth of July he published an ordinance which became, for the entire diocese, a source of much joy and relief; it was the first step towards the required solution. By this act, the Bishop instituted a commission of inquiry to examine in detail the extraordinary events of Lourdes,—apparitions and cures, and to prepare the decision it was expedient to proclaim. Thus the ecclesiastical authorities were opening a sure path to victory,—whilst on the contrary, the civil government, for having attempted, without previous examination, to settle a question which, by the way, was entirely out of its province,—was advancing day by day, by successive setbacks to absolute defeat.

From every quarter petitions were being forwarded to Emperor Napoleon III begging him to annul the arbitrary and tyrannical measures of the prefect of Tarbes. One of these read as follows:

"In the name of the rights of conscience, Sire, allow the faithful to go and pray at the Grotto, if they so desire; in the name of simple humanity, allow the sick to go there and seek their recovery, if such is their hope; in the name of liberty of mind, allow those who seek life through study and observation to go and discover either error or truth."

Such language was too sincere not to impress the sovereign's mind. He was then vacationing at the popular resort of Biarritz, on the Atlantic coast. There he was visited by many distinguished personages whose reports on Lourdes gave him a clearer idea of the state of affairs in that locality than the impassioned controversies in the press. He quickly understood that his government was making a serious mistake in meddling so stupidly in a purely religious affair in which the Church alone possessed authority and competency. By this silly indiscretion, the minister, the prefect, and their agents were simply heaping discredit upon the government.

Such were the actual dispositions of the monarch when, one day, news of fresh vexatious measures which the department had adopted were brought to his attention. With an evident air of displeasure, and without waiting for the end of the interview, he impatiently scribbled a few lines and summoned his secretary: "Take this to the telegraph office at once," said he. It was a brief despatch to the prefect of Tarbes, ordering him in the name of the Emperor to lift the mandate on the Grotto of Lourdes, and to allow the people to enjoy their liberty. For the unfortunate prefect this message came as a thunderbolt; by every conceivable means, by the most powerful influences, did he endeavor to obtain the cancellation of the order,—but all in vain. The Emperor, annoyed over the delay, despatched a second message, and the prefect obeyed.

On the third day of October a proclamation was issued at Lourdes, announcing the annulment of the order of June eighth. The commissary suffered the cruel humiliation of presiding himself at the removal of the fences and palisades which he had ordered erected less than four months previously.

This act of justice and reparation filled the inhabitants of Lourdes with intense emotion. The multitudes, composed of all classes of society, travelled back and forth on the road to the Grotto. Before the rocks of Massabielle, thousands of faithful were on their knees; everybody sang hymns, prayed, and drank at the

miraculous fountain. Once more the faithful were free,
—God had conquered.

A few weeks afterwards the prefect of Tarbes was
transferred to Grenobles; he exchanged Our Lady of
Lourdes, the Virgin with a smile for Our Lady of
La Salette, the Virgin of tears. Can we not perceive
in this strange incident one of those ironies by which
Divine Providence laughs at those who would measure
themselves with Him? *"Qui habitat in coelis iridebit
eos"* (Ps. ii. 4) The prefect of Tarbes had often remarked: "If I had been prefect of Isère at the time of
this so-called apparition of La Salette, I soon would
have mastered the situation and that legend would have
enjoyed the same fate as this one in Lourdes is going to
enjoy; all this silliness will still be a thing of the past."
But in the Alps as in the Pyrenees, it was always the
good Mother of Mercy,—and he will soon become
aware of it. As for the commissary, he was ordered
to a new field at Avignon.

Let it be said that no one ever favored the work of
Lourdes as these two men,—they who had labored so
hard to annihilate it; they furnished the element necessary to the triumph of truth and justice, that is,—
contradiction. Thanks to them the work of Lourdes
has been rewarded most magnificently with an authentic
homage from all the interested sciences: chemistry,
geology, and medicine. Indeed, the works of God can
well dispense with the certificates of men,—but we,
poor mortals, need them in order to strengthen our

faith against our ignorance and to defend it against its enemies. Thanks once more to them, this work can face, now and forever, the contradictions and sarcasms of both pride and impiety; they have succeeded in placing it, at their own expense and much against their will, in a most unassailable position. Unconsciously, those two functionaries became the collaborators of the Blessed Virgin in her work; for that reason our good Mother favored them with her protection; both died, filled with deep religious convictions, a priest at their side and a crucifix on their lips. And such was the case with the mayor of Lourdes, the procurator and the majority of the official opponents who figured at the outset. Such was the vengeance of our Heavenly Queen who, in different apparitions, had requested to pray for sinners.

INVOCATION

Hail, Mary.

"O Mary, it is through thee that those who, in the first instance were thy adversaries, received the grace of conversion; grant us the strength of forgiving those who actually injure us or wish us harm, and of proving ourselves the worthy children of the one whom the Church calls 'The Mother of Mercy.'

"Our Lady of Lourdes, pray for us."

CHAPTER XXVII

EPISCOPAL DECLARATION AND FIRST PROCESSION

WHEN calm and tranquillity were once more established in the region the commission appointed by the Bishop of Tarbes began its operations. The eminent men, both priests and laymen, who composed it started their investigation at Lourdes. Bernadette appeared before them and underwent a long interrogatory. A vast number of witnesses were summoned and were questioned most minutely on all that pertained to the child and to the apparitions. Nothing was overlooked; the Grotto was carefully examined as well as the ground from which had sprung the miraculous fountain. All the cures effected by means of this water were studied most scrupulously; only the most precise and incontestable facts were accepted. In view of the impossibility of studying every miracle,—for their number reached the hundreds, thirty of the more remarkable ones were chosen and closely scrutinized,—the investigators even taking the pains of visiting every department of the region where cures had been wrought. Two eminent physicians accompanied them:—Dr. Dozous of Lourdes and Dr. Bergès, professor at the Faculty of Medecine at Montpellier; these men controlled all the testimonies,—gathered with such scientific severity as to give the findings of the commission a basis of solidity. This preparatory work lasted many months. A detailed report was presented to Bishop Laurence who, though fully convinced of the supernatural character of the apparitions and cures, preferred, before giving it his own episcopal sanction that it receive the sanction of time.

Three more years elapsed after which he ordered a second inquest. This one was as thorough as the first which, by the way, received full confirmation since not one witness withdrew his first testimony or contested facts already registered. It is evident, therefore, that after such prolonged delays nobody ever dreamed of accusing the ecclesiastical authorities of hastiness. It was then only that the wise Bishop rendered the judgment that was expected of him. In this solemn act, accompanied by a pastoral letter of distinguished eloquence and merit, he declared: "First, that the Immaculate Mary, Mother of God, had in reality appeared to Bernadette Soubirous on the eleventh day of February, 1858, and on succeeding days to the number of eighteen times in the Grotto of Massabielle, near the city of Lourdes. Second, that the devotion to "Our Lady of the Grotto of Lourdes" was authorized in his diocese. Third, that, in response to the express wishes of the Blessed Virgin, a sanctuary would be erected on the grounds of the Grotto. This act was dated January 18, 1862. In the name of the diocese, Bishop Laurence bought from the city of Lourdes the Grotto, the land

FIRST PROCESSION

Organized in 1864 on the occasion of the blessing of the statue of Our Lady of Lourdes

that surrounds it, and the entire group of Massabielle cliffs; later he acquired the Savy Prairie.

It was not long before work began in earnest. The Grotto was left intact but the approaches were considerably transformed; the mill with its canal were obliterated and the bed of the Gave was pushed back. The Grotto was closed by an iron grating and a golden lamp was suspended from its ceiling. To receive the vast quantities of candles left by the pilgrims, many votive stands were installed but they often proved inadequate. Just outside this inclosure a number of bronze faucets facilitated the drinking and gathering of the miraculous water. In the meantime an army of workmen were erecting upon the summit of the rock, just over the Grotto, the sanctuary requested by Mary. The soul of this vast enterprise was the valiant Curé of Lourdes, Abbé Peyramale. Frequently one could see him encouraging the workmen and attending to every detail. He longed for the realization of the Virgin's twofold desire, for it was to him that the message had been conveyed. The chapel was in course of construction; but, when could he organize the first procession? At last he was given a foretaste of this happy moment after two years of strenuous labors amid difficulties that one would have judged insurmountable. The occasion of this feast was to be the blessing of the statue of Our Lady of Lourdes (the gift of the Misses de Lacour, from Chasselay, Rhône), which was to be placed in the niche of the apparitions. An eminent sculptor from Lyons, Mr. Joseph Fabisch, was busily engaged designing it according to the descriptions of Bernadette, with a scrupulous respect for the smallest details such as were furnished by the visionary. He carved it from a select block of the choicest Carrara marble; his whole soul as well as his artistic genius went out to this statue, resulting in a universally admired masterpiece. And yet, it is related that when Bernadette saw it, she was so disappointed that never again did she cast her eyes upon it, so inferior did it appear to the divine model her eyes had so often contemplated. The celebration was fixed for April 4, 1864. Following is the magnificent description given by Mr. Henri Lasserre:

"The weather was magnificent; the rejuvenated April sun had risen and was advancing under a canopy of azure, a pure cloudless sky. The city of Lourdes was bedecked with flowers, banners, garlands, and triumphal arches. In the main parish tower, in all the chapels of the city, in all the churches of the neighborhood, the great bells as well as the lesser ones rang to a merry peal. Enormous throngs had gathered for this combined feast of Heaven and earth. A procession, such as had never been witnessed by any one present, was organized at the parish church, and traversed the main arteries of the city *en route* to the Grotto of the apparitions. Troops with all the wealth and brilliancy of military display were in the lead. Immediately following were the confraternities of Lourdes, the mutual benefit societies, all the corporations of the region with their banners and their crosses raised in triumph, the Sodality of the Children of Mary whose dress trains shone with the purity of snow, the Sisters of Nevers garbed in their long black veils, the Sisters of Charity with their conspicuous white head-dress, the Sisters of St. Joseph clad in their sombre robes; the religious orders of men: the Carmelites, the Brothers of Instruction and those of the Christian Schools; the astounding multitudes of pilgrims, men, women, children, and old people. From fifty to sixty thousand men forming parallel columns wound their way through the flower-bedecked streets that led to the illustrious cliffs of Massabielle. At intervals, choruses of human voices and instruments reëchoed in the valley as the harmonious strains alternated with the outbursts of popular enthusiasm. Presently, drawing up the rear of this unprecedented triumphal march, surrounded by four hundred priests in clerical dress, by his Vicars-General, by the dignitaries and his cathedral chapter,— Very Reverend and Very Eminent Prelate, His Lordship Bertrand-Sévère Laurence, Bishop of Tarbes, garbed in his pontifical robes, with mitre,—his left hand grasping his gilded crosier, his right raised in solemn benediction over the heads of his beloved people. An indescribable emotion, a delirium known only to the Christian multitudes assembled under the eye of God, filled every heart. At last! after so much anguish, so many struggles and contradictions, the day of solemn triumph had come.   Tears of joy, of enthusiasm, and of love covered the features of these good people who had been moved by the breath of God."

In this stupendous celebration, so beautifully described, two people who should have occupied positions of honor were missing: Bernadette and the Pastor of Lourdes.   These elect of Mary were at this particular moment subjected to violent physical sufferings. Bernadette had been removed to the hospital, and Abbé Peyramale was at death's door in his rectory,—his attendants wondering if the joyous peals of the church bells would not, on this very day, be changed to a toll in announcement of his death.   But neither the one nor the other had as yet finished their task; God still had in store for them new labors as well as new tribulations.

INVOCATION

Hail, Mary.

"O Queen of Victory, in depriving thy dearest friends of their legitimate triumphs on earth, thou hast taught us to beware of the acute temptations of vain glory which thou hast spared them,—and to toil and suffer here upon earth, only in view of eternal victory in Heaven, where the joys are free from sorrow, the triumphs free from tears, and the rejoicings without fear of the morrow.

"Our Lady of Lourdes, pray for us."

CHAPTER XXVIII

SISTER MARIE BERNARD, (BERNADETTE)

Her Vocation—Her Life at Nevers—Her Death

In our narrative, we left Bernadette suffering in the hospital at Lourdes. She recovered from this crisis but her health remained anything but encouraging. She is now no longer a child, she has attained her twentieth year. The good Sisters of the hospice, in the hope of strengthening her weak constitution, by such means as her poor parents were unable to provide, begged the latter to allow the young girl to remain with them on the grounds of a "patient in need". Her attacks of asthma returned periodically and one day her sufferings, accentuated by suffocation, were so violent that the doctor who attended her declared her condition hopeless. She received the sacrament of Extreme Unction, drank a few sips of the water of the Grotto which had been brought to her, and immediately she felt a relief; little by little, her strength returned to her.

Bishop Forcade, the illustrious Prelate of Nevers, and Superior of the Congregation of Sisters whose motherhouse was located in his episcopal city, chanced to come about this time to Lourdes on his canonical visit to the community of the hospice. He found Bernadette in the kitchen occupied at peeling vegetables.

The saintly Prelate accosted her with paternal kindness, but interiorly, with a respect inspired by the marvelous history of this child who, eighteen times had seen and entertained the Mother of God.   After having questioned her at length touching the apparitions he said to her:

"My daughter, what have you planned for the future?"

"Bishop, just what I am doing at present," replied Bernadette, "work and pray with the Sisters, as their little servant."

"Have you ever thought of entering into their Congregation?"

"I, Bishop?   Of what good would I be?   I am so ignorant and so unfit?"

"If God calls you, my child, you will always have sufficient capacity; promise me that you will bear this in mind, that you will reflect and pray."

Bernadette thanked His Lordship and promised; then peacefully she resumed her duties of a servant. But from this very moment the thought of entering religion never left her.   After a year spent in meditation and prayer, convinced that she was answering the call of her Heavenly Friend, she begged the Mother Superior to be admitted into the Order, as a novice. Her request, having been forwarded to Nevers, was received with evident joy.   But on the eve of her departure the poor child was stricken once more and her voyage was necessarily postponed.   After many months, her health having been restored anew, she was again called to Nevers. What cruel sufferings for the dear girl when, on the eve of her departure, she paid a farewell visit to her beloved Grotto! As she pressed her lips again upon the blessed rock she burst into tears; a cry of anguish slipped from her bosom: "O my Mother, my Mother!" The Sisters who accompanied her were compelled to drag her away. Her grief was none the less when she bade farewell to her beloved parents, to her brothers and sisters, to her friends. To meet these cruel sacrifices unflinchingly she would often recall those memorable words which the Blessed Virgin addressed to her on her third apparition: "I do not promise to make you happy in this world, but in the next." She understood that this happiness beyond the grave is to be bought at the price of sufferings here on earth. Her departure was, furthermore, a source of sorrow for her native city which lost, in her, its most noble child.

Bernadette, arriving at Nevers, entered the convent of St. Gildard, July 7, 1866. On the twenty-ninth day of the same month she received the habit of a novice with the name of Sister Marie Bernard. She became for her companions in the novitiate a marvel of humility, obedience, piety, and amiability.

But the state of her health was always most uncertain. The twenty-fifth of October she vomited blood and the doctor, responding to an urgent call, found her in a desperate condition. Without delay the

Right Reverend Bishop was notified. He arrived during the night, and, as her vomiting spells continued, he immediately gave her the last sacraments. As His Lordship was about to take leave the Mother Superior said to him: "One thing breaks my heart, and that is, that our dear little Sister has neither received the veil nor pronounced her vows."

"What prevents her?" cried the Bishop, and he returned to the sick room.

"Sister Marie Bernard, that you may again see the Virgin of Lourdes in Heaven, it is expedient that you receive the habit of a professed Sister; do you so desire? Tell me by some sign that you understand me." The patient signified her willingness by a movement of her head and instantly an expression of ineffable joy filled her countenance. The Bishop thereupon performed the required ceremonies and pronounced, in the name of Bernadette, the formula of the vows; he then returned to his home broken with emotion,—firmly convinced that he would never again see her alive. The remainder of the night was calm and peaceful; she slept well and upon waking she found herself almost totally cured.

Soon she was able to enter the novitiate in order to complete her religious training; and on October 30, 1867, she renewed, this time solemnly in the chapel, the profession which she had made *In extremis* on her bed of agony. It is impossible to enter into the details of her convent life during the twelve years that she

* P. P. SOEUR MARIE BERNARD
(Bernadette)

* Her authentic autograph. P. P. signifies
By Permission

still had to spend on earth. Two offices were successively allotted to her; first, that of nurse at the hospice which was annexed to the convent and shortly after, on account of her delicate health, the office of sacristan. In both functions she was noted for her wonderful aptitude and her great zeal. Her sufferings, which were almost continuous, had never altered her character; she still preserved her childish gayety and that charming simplicity which, in her, did not exclude a rare keenness of mind.

These qualities, joined to an appealing frankness and to her southern vivacity, gave her a particular distinction and a most striking originality. For this reason, both at the convent and at the hospice, Sisters and patients, all without exception, had a most singular liking for our dear Sister Marie Bernard.

We have already touched upon the exquisite sensitiveness of her heart; accordingly, what terrible, what dangerous shocks she had to endure upon receipt of cruel news from Lourdes! In the first place, only a few months after her arrival at Nevers, on the eighth of December, 1866, came the news of her beloved mother's death; that of her father followed in 1871. Six years later, in 1877, another dear soul had passed away. This time it was the noble and devout Curé of Lourdes, the father of her soul, whom she loved as tenderly as those who had brought her into this world. Each of these sad announcements was a blow to her frail constitution.

Near the end of her life she was made to endure many other afflictions besides the asthma which had never left her. For instance, tumors, rheumatism, spitting of blood, decaying of the bones, etc.; and all these were not required to ruin so delicate a frame. Her life was a continuous martyrdom which she suffered with heroic fortitude and cheerful resignation. "I am happy to have an occasion to suffer," said she, "my happiness consists in being the victim of the Heart of Jesus." As Mary had taught her, she offered all her sufferings for the conversion of sinners. This supernatural reason alone could soothe the violence of the aspirations of this soul who for the last twenty years had suffered as an exile from Heaven. Unwillingly this state of mind was sometimes disclosed in her conversations. One day a little girl asked her:

"Was the Blessed Virgin very beautiful?"

"So beautiful," replied Bernadette, "that when we have once seen her, one longs to die to see her again."

A few days before her death, the chaplain, finding her much weakened through her sufferings said to her:

"My dear Sister, you are called upon to make the great sacrifice generously."

"What sacrifice, Father?"

"The sacrifice of your life."

"But that is not a sacrifice," she quickly retorted.

No, it was not a sacrifice,—it was a deliverance, ardently desired and patiently awaited.

At last the blessed hour has come. Surrounded by

the Sisters who sob as they pray, she waits in peace. For the last time, and with a heroic effort, she makes that grand and beautiful sign of the cross which had been taught her by the Mother of our Savior and which enraptured all who witnessed her ecstasies. She holds in her faltering hands a crucifix, at which she gazes lovingly, which she kisses repeatedly, saying: "Oh! how I love Him!" or some other pious ejaculation. Until the end she follows the prayers that are recited at her side, and it is in answer to the "Ave Maria" that she breathes her last, with these words: "Holy Mary, Mother of God." It was the sixteenth of April, 1879, on Wednesday of Easter week. She was thirty-five years and three months of age. Her obsequies were performed with majestic pomp under the presidency of the Bishop of Nevers, who was then Bishop Lelong. It was rather a triumph than an hour of mourning; the triumph of an humble child of the laboring class which Heaven had chosen for the great work of salvation and mercy of the nineteenth century.

Bernadette was buried in the chapel of St. Joseph, erected in the center of the garden, at the motherhouse of her Congregation.

INVOCATION

Hail, Mary.

"Holy Mary, Mother of God, may we die in imitation of Bernadette, with thy name and that of Jesus in our heart and upon our lips,—that we may continue to bless Them and to extol Them with the angels and the saints for all eternity.

"Our Lady of Lourdes, pray for us."

CHAPTER XXIX

THE WORK OF LOURDES

Sanctuaries—Processions—Celebrations

THE Immaculate Virgin had given Bernadette a first mission: "Go and tell the priests to build a chapel here in my honor." And the chapel was erected,—a veritable cathedral, rich as a casket of precious jewels, superb in its robe of white granite, with its slender spire thrusting high in the air the cross of salvation. But in a short space of time this sanctuary proved inadequate so a second chapel greater than the first,—the Church of the Rosary, was built at its feet, after an almost superhuman task,—the blasting away of a mountain of granite. And the ever-increasing multitudes had exclaimed with the poet: "How small are thy temples for my soul, O Lord! Fall, powerless walls, fall!" And before the Church of the Rosary, a third temple of unheard-of proportions with the canopy of Heaven for ceiling, has spread its vast auditorium between two monumental rows of colonnades: it is the Court of the Rosary. There only, can be carried out with all their fullness and solemn majesty, the ceremonies attending the most stupendous pilgrimage of this world. And the Virgin had said furthermore: "And I want people to come here in procession." We have described the first procession, that of April 4,

1864. Since then Lourdes has seen them, each year by the hundreds, unfold before her sanctuary and her Grotto their endless ranks of pilgrims. From what countries do they all hail? Rather, is there a country that has never been represented there? All the languages of the world are spoken at Lourdes,—all nations meet there to pay their respects to the Queen of the universe. Naturally the nations of Europe dominate in this stronghold of Catholicity, notably: Spain, Italy, Switzerland, Austria, Germany, Belgium, Holland, and England who send frequent and numerous contingents; and finally, France, which during the space of a century was visited four times by the Queen of Heaven; at Paris, at La Salette, at Lourdes, and at Pontmain.

There exists in the physical domain as well as in the moral, a universal law whereby a cause must correspond to the effects. What is then the first cause of this untold agitation on the part of men and objects,—the prime factor of this prodigious action which continues without interruption or diminution for so many years, with a power forever on the increase and overcoming all obstacles? There is only one answer: it is the word of a little shepherdess who claims to have seen what nobody else has seen, to have heard things that no other ears have heard. Here we have the least of causes producing the most stupendous effects! Let us explain this prodigy, if it be possible, outside of the theory of a miracle! What astounding history,—that of the development of the work of Lourdes, of which we have related the first phases,—and how it reveals to us the strength and vitality of the Catholic faith! Let us recall briefly its principal episodes as well as the most remarkable dates.

In 1872, France, still bleeding from the cruel wounds she received during the disastrous war of 1870, wished that all her provinces and her principal sanctuaries be represented at Lourdes by means of rich banners, symbolical and perpetual homage, to which were added those of many other nations. All these banners, over three hundred in number, suspended from the ceiling of the upper basilica, constitute a most unique decoration and one of priceless value. One of these banners draped in mourning stands out in relief,—that of captive Alsace. During one of the immense processions, Archbishop de Langalerie of Auch, who presided, stopped,—and with tears in his eyes, kissed it with effusion. A patriotic thrill permeated the entire gathering and on all sides tears flowed abundantly. (See Supplementary Note X, page 205.)

Four years later, in 1876, the basilica was consecrated and the statue of Our Lady of Lourdes solemnly crowned in the name of the Sovereign Pontiff, Pius IX, the glorious definer of the dogma of the Immaculate Conception. This imposing ceremony was attended by thirty-five prelates, including one cardinal, three thousand priests, and one hundred thousand faithful. At the twenty-fifth anniversary of the apparition, in 1883, the concourse of people was not inferior in number. It

was at this time that was laid the corner stone of the
Church of the Rosary, the consecration of which in
1901 constituted one of the greatest solemnities in the
history of Lourdes.   On this occasion there figured
twenty-five prelates, two cardinals, and one patriarch.

Outside of the ordinary pilgrimages, which average
one hundred and fifty a year, there have been a number
of pilgrimages composed exclusively of men,—of all
classes of society: legislators from both Houses, members of the Institute, officers of all ranks, industrial
chiefs, titled personages, laborers, and country-folks,—
whose ranks were blended into one great brotherhood
of faith, love, and prayer.   The pilgrimage of 1903
numbered sixty thousand men.   To solve the problem
of conveying to Lourdes such stupendous throngs
which follow one another uninterruptedly during eight
months of the year, the railway company of southern
France had recourse to special organizations.   The
little city of Lourdes which, at the outset, had no railway accommodation is to-day,—due to the numerous
pilgrimages, the most frequented spot of its system.
Its immense railway station receives annually in excess
of one million travelers.

And what must we think of the days at Lourdes,
with their celebrations which defy all description?   At
the early hours Masses are celebrated without interruption at the Grotto, and at all the altars of the two
basilicas and of the crypt, at those of the parish church
and of all the city chapels; everywhere Holy Com-

munion is being continually distributed to the pilgrims.
At ten o'clock a High Mass is celebrated with great
solemnity in one of the two basilicas,—oftentimes in
the open, in the Court of the Rosary. Here one is fed
with the word of God as it falls from the lips of most
distinguished orators. The afternoons are taken up
with the procession of the Blessed Sacrament; and how
natural! The true devotion to the Blessed Virgin is
necessarily based upon the devotion to Jesus, actually
present in the Holy Eucharist: "*Ad Jesum per Mariam,*
—To Jesus through Mary."

The procession starts from the Grotto. The people
are lined in two parallel columns between which advance groups of Children of Mary or of different associations, preceded by their respective banners. Then
comes the clergy,—always very numerous, with lighted
candles in hand; and lastly, the prelate, 'neath the
canopy, holding in his hands the sacred Ostensorium.
Solemn Eucharistic hymns are chanted by the entire
multitude with a penetrating accent of faith, adoration,
and love. But how inspiring this spectacle becomes
when the procession reaches the Court of the Rosary!
From all sides, carried by special bearers, young and
valiant heroes of charity, can be seen as many as
one thousand cripples. There, all the human infirmities are represented, all the diseases which resisted the
scientific efforts of medicine. Invocations are intoned
and continue without interruption;—they are the same
that were addressed to Jesus of Nazareth by the sick

and the infirm. And the celebrant slowly makes his way through this immense hospital, stopping before each cot and presenting to each patient the all-powerful Master of life and death. Now and then, a cry followed by a thousand others, reëchoes in the vast expanse: it is a dying man who is born to a new life, a cripple who rises upon his limbs, a blind woman who regains the use of her sight; it is a hideous sore which is healed, or a crippled limb that becomes normal. What emotion! What enthusiasm! And the august ceremony comes to an end with benediction of the Blessed Sacrament during which, in the silence of adoration, the vast throng remains prostrate.

During this solemn moment all hearts are moved and abundant tears are shed; it is oftentimes the hour of interior miracles. For the spiritual cures, there does not exist as in the case of other miracles, a bureau of authenticity,—they are registered only in Heaven. But one thing is certain and that is,—that no place on earth can boast of so many conversions. How many hearts in which a dying faith has been rekindled! How many others who had never possessed it and who opened wide their doors to its sweet and salutary influence! It is in the confessionals of the crypt that these happy victims of Divine grace will go, before leaving Lourdes, to exchange the burden of their sins for Divine pardon and the peace of mind which follows it.

The day, always so short, comes to an end and night spreads its sombre shades over all things. But suddenly a brilliant light springs forth; the entire basilica, from its base to the tip of its lofty spire, is resplendent with thousands of multi-colored lights which bring out its gothic lines and accentuate its brilliancy against the dark background of the heavens. Simultaneously, myriads of lights appear, and are all set in motion. The picture, from a neighboring mountain, would be that of a fantastic river of infinite curves whose luminous waves resemble those of the ocean during the phosphorescent nights of summer. And from these rolling waves there rises an immense, an overpowering harmony, one that is born of a never changing melody, one whose syllables intermingle without a discordant note,—in imitation of the solemn chant of the ocean. And what say those waves that sing? "Ave, Ave, Ave Maria!" It is the melody of love from ten thousand, twenty thousand hearts,—melody always the same, and which never repeats itself because the heart is never tired of singing it. And the impressed spectator wonders if this is a feast of Heaven or a feast of the earth.

But the feasts of this earth have an end, and this one required an ending worthy of it. When all the units of this immense procession have been massed together on the Court of the Rosary,—which now resembles a lake of stars, a signal is given and singing ceases. Presently, in the midst of this imposing silence, powerful voices intone the "Credo", which all the assistants continue in a majestic unison. What a contrast to the enthusiastic chant of the "Ave Maria!" It is now the hour of profound recollection of the Christian soul who affirms his faith, happy and proud to proclaim it in the face of Heaven and earth, on this blessed spot where each day a brilliant confirmation is given, by the miracle, to all the truths which God has revealed to His Church. How can one better sum up all the sentiments, all the impressions, all the teachings of one day at Lourdes than by the word "Credo"?

INVOCATION

Hail, Mary.

"O Queen of Heaven and earth, while the feasts of the world are frequently followed by disgust, weariness, and remorse, thy feasts and those of Jesus are sweet to the heart and beneficial to the soul; they bring with them joy and consolation, strength and hope; they are a foretaste of the eternal joys of Paradise.

"Our Lady of Lourdes, pray for us."

CHAPTER XXX

THE PILGRIMAGE OF LOURDES

*Mr. H. Lasserre and his Book—Abbé Picard and
His Works*

RELATIVE to the pilgrimage of Lourdes, there exist
two prophesies absolutely contradictory: one transmitted by Bernadette to the Curé of Lourdes, on the
part of the Celestial Lady: "I want people to come here
in procession," the other launched disdainfully from a
rostrum of a French parliament by an illustrious states-
man (Mr. Thiers): "This won't last,—pilgrimages are
out of date with us." The great orator lived long
enough to understand that in this circumstance as well
as in many others, he had been at the same time a bad
prophet and an imprudent judge. Pilgrimages are so
much up-to-date that the nineteenth century has seen
them developed to a degree unknown to the most
fervent centuries of the middle ages,—due no doubt,
to the greater facilities which we enjoy to-day, owing
to the progress of science.

In order to attain this end Divine Providence has
made use of two men whose surroundings and dispositions were absolutely different one from the other.
The first was taken from the select group which comprises Men of Letters; this man is Mr. Henri Lasserre,
talented writer, already in possession of an undeniable

MR. HENRI LASSERRE
Historian of the Works of Lourdes

literary reputation,—but very little disposed to use his pen in the interests of religion, towards which he was quite indifferent. Almighty God sent him an affliction: his eyesight became so impaired, that he was threatened with early blindness. In vain did he consult the most eminent specialists,—eventually losing all hope. In the meantime, an intimate friend, a man of distinction, and a Protestant (Mr. de Freycinet),—upon returning from the waters of Cauterets, had stopped through curiosity at Lourdes, and what he saw and heard there singularly impressed him. Without delay he related all his impressions to Mr. Lasserre and urged him at the same time to have recourse to this wonderful remedy already famous as the Water of Lourdes.

The patient, amazed at receiving such advice from such a source, resisted at first, alleging a twofold reason: lack of confidence, and especially, the obligation under which he would be in case of recovery, to change his mode of life and to impose upon himself certain privations which his weakness could not endure. His Protestant friend insisted so strenuously and with arguments so convincing that he finally won out, and without delay he wrote himself to Lourdes that some water from the Grotto be forwarded to him. After a few days, a small casket containing one quart of this water was delivered to Mr. Lasserre's address. He opened it, trembling, and falling upon his knees, he prayed God from the bottom of his heart, earnestly begging forgiveness for his guilty cowardice. Encouraged by this prayer he poured a little of the water in a cup and kneeling a second time, he cried with a loud voice: "O holy Virgin Mary, have pity upon me, and cure my moral as well as my physical blindness!" He then rubbed both eyes with a towel saturated with the water of Lourdes: "Judge for yourselves," relates he, "of my shock; I was about to say—of my terror! I had hardly touched my eyes and my forehead with this miraculous water when I felt myself absolutely cured; and it came about instantly without the ordinary transition. That very evening I went to confession, and the following morning I received Holy Communion in thanksgiving." From this day Mr. Lasserre has courageously embraced the life of a real Christian, with all its exigencies, the realization of which had so frightened him. From this moment also he became the apostle of Lourdes, consecrating to his work a vast portion of his fortune, but especially, his rare talent as a writer in order to spread its marvels. His first book on this subject created such a demand that it found its way into every nook and corner of Europe. It was translated in all the principal languages. (The first edition appeared in 1869.) Never was there a book that obtained such success or that boasted of so many editions. It was in reality the bugle call that resounded throughout the world, and to which the people responded by flying to Lourdes, there to honor and invoke the Immaculate Virgin Mary. (Henri Lasserre died, most piously, July 22, 1900.)

In order to spread and to direct this movement of wonders, Divine Providence signalled out, shortly after, another apostle who had received in an eminent degree the gifts of faith and zeal, of eloquence and organization; this apostle was Abbé Picard, Superior General of the Augustinians of the Assumption. In 1871, following the disaster which had befallen France, —as a means of bringing about both her moral and Christian recovery, he founded the admirable "Association of Our Lady of Salvation," which comprises in its program all the works of piety and social activity, necessary to obtain this end. (The seat of this association is in Paris, 4, Avenue de Breteuil.) Among these works pilgrimages occupied a prominent position. It was in 1873 that the special committee, with the approbation and encouragement of Pius IX, despatched towards Lourdes its first train under the name of National Pilgrimage. The following year a number of trains became necessary,—and from year to year their numbers were multiplied. On the occasion of the twenty-fifth anniversary pilgrimage in 1897,[1] there were eighteen trains, twenty in 1899, twenty-six in 1906, and thirty-three in 1913 and 1914. Simultaneously, in all dioceses of France and in many foreign dioceses as well, similar institutions were established under the same organization and with the same progress. And to think that pilgrimages are out of date!

[1] It was on this occasion that, following an impassioned allocution by Abbé Picard, forty-one sick patients rose successively from their cots, amid a most indescribable enthusiasm on the part of the pilgrims.

The National Pilgrimage,—and in this, it was imitated by all others, did not limit its endeavors in convoying to Lourdes capable pilgrims only; but, in accordance with a touching and most sublime inspiration, it organized special convoys of the sick in the poorer classes, assuming at the same time all expenses of travel, of medical attendance, of board and lodging. For this purpose a yearly subscription is taken up, increasing steadily each year. The first year, that is, in 1873, it produced 320 francs; 4,961 in 1876; 10,184 in 1877; 29,600 in 1878; 46,122 in 1879; and to-day it averages 70,000 francs. Is this not a veritable outburst of piety and charity? Is it not true that all that concerns Lourdes is endowed with a miraculous character? All these contributions have enabled the organizers to convey to the Virgin of Massabielle, by means of the National Pilgrimage, from 1873 to 1908,—28,730 sick patients (this amount would be tripled if we added the number of sick brought under the same conditions by the different diocesan pilgrimages), taken from the ranks of the poor and of this number a good proportion received miraculous favors. This prodigious work constitutes a brilliant testimony in behalf of the miracles of Lourdes, as much on the part of the subscribers as that of the sick themselves.

And no less eloquent testimony is the institution of stretcher-bearers and hospitallers,—a new order of chivalry, under the title of "Hospitality of Our Lady of Salvation." Recruiting for this twofold legion is done in a great measure among society people. These are wealthy and generous volunteers who, during the best months of the year, come to Lourdes and, at their own expense, serve in the capacity of valets or servants of the poor. It is a way of theirs, by means of their money and their work, to dispel the social hatred which divides the classes. Isn't this a more sublime democracy than to squander their income in boisterous or expensive saunterings? Behold those valiant young men, decorated with their leather braces, the instruments and insignia of their functions, and those noble ladies adorned with the white apron of their office! All are found at their respective posts, at the railroad station, at the arrival of the sick,—the ladies, to give them with the most delicate affections, their words of encouragement and their help;—the men, to carry them away on stretchers to the different hotels or hospices. This difficult task will be the lot of these noble men every day from the early morning hours until night, under a burning sun or in the rain, carrying the sick to the Grotto or to the baths, and bringing them back; while the hospitallers in the meantime, wait upon them with indefatigable devotedness.

They can be seen vieing with another body which bears a glorious name,—very like those who console the afflicted and relieve the sick,—I refer to the "Little Sisters of the Assumption." Their congregation, of a recent foundation, has acquired world-wide renown and has extended its influence throughout the old and the new world,—and all this without apparent effort. It is through sheer kindness, through constant devotedness that the Little Sister has commanded the attention and admiration of everybody. From Paris to Lourdes it is she who cares for the sick on the train, assuming thereby the greatest of fatigue, accomplishing all alone a piece of work rendered doubly repugnant by the closeness of the quarters and the lack of accommodations. In the city of miracles it is entirely different; the Little Sister vanishes. At the most can she be found at the "Permanance,"—for her modesty forbids that she appear in public even for a work of charity. What a spectacle and what an example! It defies description,—one must see it; nothing but faith and Christian charity can produce such wonders.

And should we be astonished that such heroic acts, such increasing devotedness which we find in this atmosphere of piety and prayer at Lourdes, would be so frequently rewarded by miraculous cures?

Abbé Picard, who was the founder and inspiration of these admirable institutions, died a saintly death in exile at Rome, in 1903. But his works survive him. The cloak of Elijah was recovered by Elisha, imbued with his spirit,—and the pilgrimage of Lourdes, which he vivified during the lapse of thirty years, continues its beneficent inspiration and its salutary action, with an ever-increasing intensity.

The immense number of pilgrims who come to Lourdes from every quarter of the universe represent but a very small minority of those who honor and invoke our Lady of Lourdes. How many would like to respond in person to her call: "I wish to see people here," (third apparition), and who will never be in a position to see this desire realized! Distance, the lack of time and resources constitute, for the majority, really insurmountable obstacles. Those who have had the good fortune to make this pilgrimage, would love to repeat it: whoever sees Lourdes longs to see it again. For this reason, in order to encourage so ardent and so universal a devotion, Catholic piety has multiplied Lourdes. Not only is the charming image of the Immaculate Virgin venerated in most of the churches of the universe, but in many localities we find reproduced the Grotto of the apparitions as well as the sanctuaries erected at Lourdes. Lourdes is everywhere, on every shore, on every island of the globe.

You will find Lourdes at the Vatican, and the imprisoned Pope who has never known the happiness of praying before the Grotto of Massabielle, has at least the consolation of possessing a faithful copy of the same in his gardens. Spain, Italy, Belgium, England, the United States and many other countries have fashioned Grottoes or built churches in honor of our Pyrenean Queen. One may find these shrines in the heart of the Mussulman's domain, even at the doors of Constantinople, at Fery-Keuy where miracles have been performed, in Mexico, in Chili, in the center of Asia and Africa, in every land visited by the Catholic missionary.   Everywhere this pilgrimage exists, and oftentimes the good Mother has rewarded the faith of her children by the most brilliant favors.   This devotion is as truly catholic as the Holy Church of Jesus Christ, that is, universal.

INVOCATION

Hail, Mary.

"Our Lady of Lourdes, in appearing to Bernadette on the rocks of Massabielle, thou hast caused to shine in the eyes of this child a ray of Heaven, one whose reflection continues to enrapture our happy pilgrims.   Grant us the grace of always remaining faithful to Jesus, that our laborious pilgrimage here on earth may lead us to that glorious Paradise, where we hope to rejoice with thee for all eternity.

"Our Lady of Lourdes, pray for us."

CHAPTER XXXI

LOURDES AND THE MIRACLE

Pierre de Rudder—Gabriel Gargam

Our Lord, during His mortal life, performed miracles and He Himself has told us why: "The works themselves which I do, give testimony of Me, that the Father hath sent Me." (Joan. v, 36.) "If I do not the works of My Father, believe Me not; but if I do, though you will not believe Me, believe the works." (Joan. x, 37, 38.) The miracle was therefore in His mind, as a letter of credit confirming His mission, a guarantee of the truth of His word, a proof of His divinity. In fact, the miracle being a derogation of the laws of creation, none but the Creator can be the cause of it,—for the legislator alone is master of his law. In presence of such a fact we are forcibly compelled to say, as the diviners of Egypt in the face of the plagues which visited that country, "This is the finger of God" (Ex. viii; 19); or again with the Psalmist: "This is the Lord's doing" (Ps. cxvii; 23). To this first admission of common sense is immediately added another: "God, Who is truth itself, cannot perform a miracle in favor of error." One must believe the word of a thaumaturgist: "Jesus Christ said that He is God; therefore, He is." This was an irrefutable logic against which the stubborn Pharisees fought in vain. This same argument has always preserved its merits and produced the same effects. For nineteen centuries the miracle, the abode of which is the Church, continues to affirm the divinity of the works of Jesus Christ.

Notwithstanding the opposition of the Pharisees of all ages, true to their forefathers, the miracle has always compelled them to remain silent or to talk foolishly. What these modern Pharisees did not invent to explain, outside of the supernatural, some stupendous facts whose existence they could not deny! They had recourse to so-called scientific theories which they decorated with such pompous names as: hypnose, auto-suggestion, psychotherapy, and others equally brilliant, and they only succeeded in accentuating still more their powerlessness, giving thereby more publicity to their defeat. Oh! how perfect is the realization of this saying of our Lord: "Everyone that exalteth himself shall be humbled." (Luke xviii; 14.) It is the eternal punishment of the proud man who defies God or His works.

Let us recall the cures that we have already related,—for instance, those of Bourriette and of the Bouhohorts child. Is there room for the hypnose theory in the instantaneous restoration of an eye rendered useless twenty years previously, or for auto-suggestion in the return to life of a two-year-old child after an immersion of fifteen minutes in ice-cold water? These two facts alone would suffice to establish beyond all reasonable doubt the miraculous character of the water of Lourdes. And it is by thousands that we count the cures, scientifically authenticated by medical affidavits. The wonderful multiplicity of these cures prevents each one in particular from enjoying the publicity it would deserve, were it completely isolated; it is lost in the mass, as the particular sound of each instrument is in an orchestra of which it helps to augment the volume. However, some of these cures, owing to more remarkable circumstances which accompanied them, have been spared this inevitable oblivion; such are the celebrated cases of Pierre de Rudder and of Gabriel Gargam, which we will describe.

On February 16, 1867, a laborer by the name of Pierre de Rudder from the town of Jabbeke near Ostend, Belgium, had a leg crushed by the fall of a tree. The doctor found that the fracture of both bones, the tibia and the fibula, just below the knee was a complete one. A complication soon set in, through the appearance of purulent and gangrenous ulcers,— another large ulcer spreading over the top of the foot. In turn, many physicians were called to treat the patient,—but all without exception declared the disease incurable, each one proposing as sole alternative, the amputation of the limb. De Rudder steadfastly refused. After a short period, a fragment of bone was loosened in the wound and it became necessary to remove it with the result that the two extremities became separated by at least one inch. This situation continued for eight years causing the unfortunate man constant, and at times, most intolerable sufferings.

On April 7, 1875, Pierre accompanied by his wife undertook a pilgrimage to the sanctuary of Our Lady of Lourdes which had been established for some time at Oestacher, near Gand, and which had already become quite popular in that region. The voyage, partly by rail and partly by team, was a most distressing one. The poor cripple, dragging himself along on two crutches, finally reached the Grotto. It was pitiful to watch him. When he walked, his afflicted limb, to which no device had been attached, swung back and forth, as it was held simply by the flesh. After having taken a little of the water of Lourdes,—for the Grotto is never without it, he circled the rustic sanctuary twice, always praying in the meantime, and then sat facing the statue of the Blessed Virgin. Suddenly he rose, and as one who has lost his mind and without any help whatsoever he went and knelt before the venerated image. He was cured; he rose and walked easily and without pain. Many witnesses were able at that very moment to certify that the bones had been reunited and to examine the two scars which indicated the position of the sores. This sudden recovery produced a tremendous sensation in Belgium where it commanded the attention of the medical faculty. For a great number of freethinkers, including one of the physicians who had treated de Rudder, it became an occasion of a sincere and public conversion.

Pierre de Rudder lived twenty-three years after his cure; he died of pneumonia, March 22, 1898, at the age of seventy-five years. The following year, at the instigation of many physicians, the body was exhumed and the legs amputated at the knees. The two bones of the left leg showed clearly where the fractures had occurred and they were found similar in length to those of the right leg notwithstanding the extraction of a fragment of the tibia before the cure. They have been preserved as a mute testimony. Pilgrims at Lourdes can examine, on a table at the Bureau of Information, an exact reproduction in bronze of these miraculously reconstructed bones.

The case of Gabriel Gargam is no less remarkable. This was in 1899. He was a handsome young man of twenty-nine, active and remarkably intelligent. He had graduated with honor at the Lyceum of Angoulême where he had won a Bachelor's diploma but where he had also lost his faith. Having obtained employment at the postal service he entertained the legitimate ambition of advancing in this direction, and in consequence he was being prepared for special examinations. On the seventeenth of December, the Bordeaux-Paris Express to which he had been assigned having accidentally slowed up was telescoped by another train just outside of Angoulême. The casualties were terrific. Gabriel was found at seven o'clock in the morning, lying in a snow bank, thirty-five feet from the track,— his body a mass of wounds. The shock had also produced in his organism the most serious disorders; he was consequently in a dying condition when removed to the hospital.

We omit the phases and the progress of the young man's confinement and are brought to July 2, 1901. On that day the Railroad Company was ordered to pay the young man a heavy indemnity coupled with a pension for life; but in view of his condition, they consoled themselves with the thought that they would be soon freed of this burden. After spending twenty months at the hospital, and having lost all hope, the patient requested that he be taken home to die amongst his own people. His pious mother never ceased praying for her unfortunate son,—caring more for his soul than for his body. At that period the National Pilgrimage to Lourdes was being organized. Mrs. Gargam pleaded with her son to take part in it. He naturally resisted at first but finally consented in order to please his mother. It was a hazardous trip. The lower portion of his body was completely paralyzed, the upper being so weak that at the slightest shock the patient would experience a fainting spell and would lapse into a sort of coma. It was with great difficulty that food could be administered to him, and this only through a tube into the œsophagus. For his comfort, a special stretcher with a soft mattress was prepared. His mother, a friend of the family, and a nurse accompanied him, as also his unbelief. And so on the morning of August 20, as the train reached the outskirts of Lourdes, his mother pointed out to him the great Christus which dominates Mt. Calvary, saying: "Behold Lourdes! Salute Christ and beg him to cure you! " For sole answer Gabriel turned his head away. Still, in order to comply with his mother's wish, he went to confession before leaving and at the Grotto he received Holy Communion (not so much as a faithful believer but as a man of honor), for he had promised his mother that he would. And yet, after this communion where faith had played so small a part, something strange came over him; he suddenly felt within himself a strong desire to pray; the grace of God had entered his soul and flooded it with light and life. During the afternoon he was taken to the baths and dipped into the miraculous water and from there to the Court of the Rosary for the procession of the Blessed Sacrament. He had no sooner reached the spot than he went into a faint, his features became livid and his body as cold as a corpse. All thought that he was breathing his last. At this particular moment the Blessed Sacrament reached his cot and behold! our patient opens his eyes and returns to life. He raises his body with the aid of his hands but falls backwards; he tries again and this time he stands erect, barefooted, in his white night robe,—the picture of one emerging from his tomb enshrouded in his white linen. He wishes to walk behind the Blessed Sacrament but he is prevented and is forced to lie down. He was totally cured though all hesitated to believe it. The paralysis had left him and he once more felt the need of food and drink.

Since then Gabriel Gargam has enjoyed perfect health and each year he visits Lourdes in thanksgiving. His activity is most wonderful; as voluntary hospitaller, he is unsurpassed; whole days are spent with the sick, the hard work of the baths being especially relished by him; he bathes them, he prays with them, caring but little for fatigue or repulsion. Gargam is a middle-aged man of exquisite appearance and refined personality; he wears a light Van Dyke beard; the top of his head is bald,—it is the only relic his infirmities have left him.

INVOCATION

Hail, Mary.

"O most powerful Virgin, Our Lady of Miracles, be thou forever blessed for thy infinite benefits for so many unfortunate creatures who have had recourse to thy inexhaustible bounties; be thou especially blessed for the precious help thou givest to our faith in vindicating it from the attacks and sarcasms of its enemies.

"Our Lady of Lourdes, pray for us."

CHAPTER XXXII

LOURDES AND THE POPES

Pius IX—Leo XIII—Pius X

ONE day, our Lord in the presence of all His disciples, addressed this solemn word to Peter: "Thou art Peter, and upon this rock I will build My Church. . . . And whatsoever thou shalt bind upon earth, it shall be bound also in Heaven,—and whatsoever thou shalt loose on earth shall be loosed also in Heaven" (Matt. xvi; 18, 19). It was the investiture of a truly divine power, given to one whom Christ had constituted visible head of His Church. In virtue of this power, Peter and his successors will enjoy, until the end of time, absolute and universal control over all doctrines, as well as all that pertains to them. All that they condemn is bad, all that they approve is good,—and their decisions are infallible rules of truth, matters of faith. No idea in the philosophical or religious order can escape their approval. Such is the extent of this power that it controls even the communications of God with man,—to such a degree, that to be of some value to the faithful they must receive the sanction of the Popes. Revelations and miracles are no exception to this rule and in order to be styled such, the approbation of the sovereign Pontiff is requisite.

This approbation has not failed the work of Lourdes, being given with such superabundance and grandeur as to place this work ahead of all other divine manifestations of this nature. No doubt this approbation does not proclaim the fact of the apparitions at Lourdes a dogma or a truth of defined faith; but if it does not enjoy this supreme solemnity and this effect, it nevertheless imposes itself with such authority that to resist it would be at the same time stupid and foolhardy. When one considers how slow and prudent the Church is in the examination of all such matters, to what serious investigations she submits them, her final decision constitutes law in face of common sense and human faith,—to the exclusion of all uncertainty.

We have noticed previously with what severity the Bishop of Tarbes applied, from the outset, this method of investigation. It is only after an examination of three years that he finally decided to proclaim his judgment. The authority of the Pope was not requisite for it was simply a question of a fact and not of a doctrine which requires the infallible magistracy of the Church. But if no definition was proclaimed on this subject, numerous public acts have clearly outlined the attitude of three Popes who have governed the Church since the apparitions: Pius IX, Leo XIII, and Pius X.

The first document that we find is a brief of praise and commendation addressed to the historian of Lourdes, Mr. Henri Lasserre, dated December 4, 1869. In this, Pius IX declares the "the apparition

THE GROTTO
As it appears to-day

of the Immaculate Conception in the Grotto of Lourdes is a fact of brilliant truth." In 1874 he elevated the chapel of Lourdes to the rank of Minor Basilica, and offered his portrait in mosaic as a decoration for its façade. Two years after, in 1876, he delegated Cardinal Guibert, Archbishop of Paris, to consecrate it in his name, and the same year he sent Bishop Meglia under the title of Apostolic Nuncio to crown the statue of the glorious Virgin. The following year he presented to the Immaculate Mary, Our Lady of Lourdes, the golden rose which is blessed each year by the Pope (this blessing takes place on the fourth Sunday of Lent, before Mass), and offered to the queens and princesses of the earth who are worthy of this favor.

In the Vatican there are abundant souvenirs of Lourdes. In the Pope's study can be seen the statue of the Immaculate; another serves as decoration for the magnificent hall of the Immaculate Conception; and, in his private oratory is found a rich wainscotted enamel representing the apparition of March twenty-fifth,—a gift of Bishop Langenieux, then Bishop of Tarbes. And again in his garden, the Pope possesses a perfect facsimile of the celebrated Grotto; and on his daily promenades he often stops and offers up a "Hail Mary" to the Virgin. There also is located a fountain filled with the water of Lourdes; at times the Pope has some of this water carried to the sick, and he uses it himself to soothe his own infirmities.

Leo XIII inherited this devotion of Pius IX and

proved it time and again. It is in his name that the corner stone of the Church of the Rosary was laid in 1883 by Cardinal Desprez, Archbishop of Toulouse; that this sanctuary was blessed in 1889 by Cardinal Richard, Archbishop of Paris, appointed for the occasion Legate of the Pope; and finally, that it was consecrated in 1901, by Cardinal Langenieux, Archbishop of Reims, also vested with the title and insignia of Apostolic Delegate. It is also Leo XIII who approved in 1890 both the Office and the Mass of the Apparition of Lourdes and which his successor, Pius X, proclaimed obligatory for the entire world (November 13, 1907).

Pius X, in imitation of his predecessors, developed an intense devotion to our Lady of Lourdes. He accepted with ineffable joy an offer to replace in the Vatican gardens, by a monumental Grotto surmounted by a facsimile of the basilica,—the modest Grotto already existing, and when the work was completed he himself presided at its solemn dedication, March 28, 1905, in the presence of the Pontifical Court and a vast concourse of people. This sanctuary was also for our saintly Pope the object of many a promenade, or rather of many a pious pilgrimage. Unable to come to Lourdes personally, he was represented at the jubilee celebration, in 1908, by a legate. To Cardinal Lecot, Archbishop of Bordeaux, was confided the mission of inaugurating the solemnities in his name on the eleventh day of February, 1908,—the fiftieth anniversary of the first apparition.

Amongst other spiritual favors let us mention the famous indulgence of three hundred days applicable to the souls of purgatory, which all the faithful can gain each time that they pronounce the following invocation: "Our Lady of Lourdes, pray for us."

This special devotion of the Popes for Our Lady of Lourdes has, without a doubt, a distinct cause which is added to this sentiment so universal in the Church, called the Devotion to the Blessed Virgin,—a sentiment particularly strong and profound in the city of the Popes. And what is this cause? It is that the Blessed Virgin came to Lourdes to convey to the world God's answer to the most important religious act of modern times, that is,—to the proclamation of the dogma of the Immaculate Conception of Mary, solemnly defined at Rome, December 8, 1854, by Pope Pius IX. This answer, supported by the irresistible argument of the miracle, is a striking confirmation of the Pontifical decree,—especially, as it constitutes an efficacious remedy against the evils of our age: naturalism, rationalism, and materialism. Owing to government schools, to literature, and to the theatre, the public mind became more and more saturated with these odious doctrines,—distinguished one from another by the slightest shades, and which converge necessarily to the negation of all religious truths. They discard revelation altogether: the fall of man and its deplorable consequences, concupiscence and sin, reparation of sin by the Incarnation, the Redemption, the Church and

Her Sacraments; and finally they reject the eternal sanction in the other world: Heaven and hell. No belief can possibly subsist in a mind infected by any one of these errors: it is man without faith, without religion, without God.

At Lourdes, the Blessed Virgin came to vindicate the truth of a conquering word: "I am the Immaculate Conception,"—that is, as Pius IX defined it,—"of all the children of Adam, I alone have been exempt from original sin with which all other descendants are born." To this dogma as a primary link, is attached the entire chain of the other dogmas. It is the teaching of the Church confirmed by the miracle, because inasmuch as it is the work of God the miracle cannot uphold error,— it is the divine witness of truth.

The Church of Jesus Christ, as in the days of the Apostles when she was established upon the ruins of conquered paganism, has received at Lourdes in this century of negation and decadence, an impetus of energy,—an evident sign of a future of reparation and uplifting. It is spring which announces and promises the return of summer.

And this explains why the Popes and the bishops, the clergy and the faithful have saluted, with so many acclamations of joy and gratitude, Mary to whom the Church has always attributed her victories over error: *"Cunctas haereses sola interemisti in universo mundo.—* (It is thou who hast given the death blow to all the heresies of the world.)"

INVOCATION

Hail, Mary.

"O Immaculate Virgin, be thou forever blessed for the wonderful bounties thou hast brought from Heaven in visiting this world; thou hast strengthened our faith, enlivened our hope, enkindled in our hearts the flame of charity. Confirm, O Mother most amiable, all that thou hast done in our midst; we beg this for our country, for all the nations where the name of thy divine Son Jesus is known, worshipped and loved.

"Help of Christians, Our Lady of Lourdes, pray for us."

OUR LADY OF LOURDES

Words by
Rt. Rev. H. T. HENRY

Music by
Rev. JOSEPH A. FREDETTE

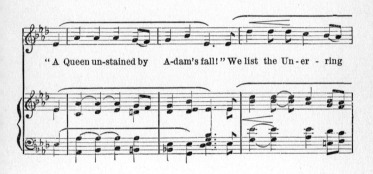

" A Queen un-stained by   A-dam's fall! " We list the Un - er - ring

Teach-er's voice: In   Ma - ry's tri-umph,   shall not all   The

faith - ful earth re-joice? A - ve,   a - ve,   a - ve Ma-ri -

a,   A - ve,   a - ve,   a - ve Ma - ri -   a.

Anon the glorious visions came
To Bernadette, of peasant kin,
And Mary's lips themselves proclaim
    Her sinless origin.

O happy Grot, O Blessed Rock,
Thus dowered high with heavenly wealth,
What wonder that ye should unlock
    Your grateful streams of health?

What wonder that from every land
The pilgrim hosts should seek the Sign
And gather in a suppliant band
    Before your healing shrine?

The gracious Virgin thus hath willed
To grant her clients' long desire:
The grateful hosts, their hopes fulfilled,
    With happy songs retire.

O loving Mother, bring relief
To deeper woes!   Implore the gift
Of Life that knoweth ne'er a grief,
    Beyond the starry lift!

SUPPLEMENTARY
NOTES

I

WITNESSES AND TESTIMONIES

OVER sixty years have elapsed since the apparitions described in this book have taken place, and by this time the witnesses have probably all disappeared. But the enemies of the supernatural cannot invoke this argument against the faith of a Christian under pretext that control of these facts is no longer possible. It was easy when Mr. Henri Lasserre published his book only a few years after the events occurred. "I wish to declare everything," writes he, "while the witnesses are still living; I gave their names and addresses that they might be questioned, that the adversaries might undertake a new inquest following mine, which would strengthen my own work. I was desirous that each reader might examine my assertions and thereby pay homage to the truth. I hoped that I might be confused and dishonored, if I lied." Such a counter-inquest, challenged by the eloquent writer, was frequently made,— for there was never an event which stirred up such intense interest and curiosity, which excited so much passion, occasioned so many polemics, and inspired so many articles, hostile or otherwise, such as newspaper editorials or reviews, books or pamphlets.

As a result of all this turmoil, the belief in the authenticity of the apparitions of Lourdes increased steadily without ever having experienced the slightest interruption. The witnesses may disappear,—the testimonies remain; and among these testimonies is there one more eloquent and more decisive than the very existence of the pilgrimage? There can be no effect without a cause. Behold a beautifully developed oak! Who would dare deny that this old oak sprang from an acorn, under the supposition that the seed which gave it birth had long since disappeared without even leaving a trace of its own self!

II

ONE WITNESS

One of the most important witnesses of the apparitions of Lourdes, who became one of their most authorized historians,—J. B. Estrade, former registrar, —died in the Lord January 1, 1909, in his eightieth year, at Bazas (Gironde), where he lived ever since his retirement.

The Right Reverend Bishop of Nevers instituted a commission to inform the process of beatification of Bernadette, the members of which proceeded to Bazas, at the close of the year 1908, for the purpose of questioning Mr. Estrade relative to the apparitions and the visionary. Unfortunately the venerable old gentleman had been reduced to such a state of physical and intellectual decrepitude that little satisfaction could be hoped for. He was hopelessly confined to his bed and had become speechless; his death appeared imminent. The members of the commission, apparently disconcerted, were permitted nevertheless to see him. And behold! the dying man emerges from his torpor and submits without fatigue to an interview of two hours. The night that followed proved curative and the next day he was able to rise. Without the least aid he donned his Sunday clothes in honor of the Blessed Virgin to whom he was going to render a last, a most solemn testimony. It is in this state that he received his visitors,—with the same amiable distinction. In a long interview he related with great precision the entire chain of apparitions and presented the commission with a vast quantity of notes written by himself in 1858, and which had never been published.

III

BERNADETTE AFTER DEATH

The day after Bernadette's death, her body lay in state in the convent chapel. For three days the population of Nevers and of the surrounding country pressed about her remains to contemplate those features rendered more beautiful in death. The throngs were at times so great that the chapel became taxed to its capacity and moving files were resorted to. Many nuns were continually occupied in receiving objects from the faithful and in applying them to the virginal body of the deceased. When she was laid in her casket it was noticed with admiration that her hands and feet had preserved their natural softness and that her body had suffered no alteration whatsoever. Thirty years and six months later, near the latter part of September, 1909, the canonical commission appointed to prepare her cause ordered the casket opened and the remains of the humble friend of the Blessed Virgin were found to be in a perfect state of preservation. "One can hardly conceive," wrote the "Univers" on the subject, "a greater contradiction of the laws of nature than the fact of a corpse, committed to earth but preserved from rottenness,—natural outcome after the decomposition of a body when life has left it."

The venerable remains were transferred to a new casket and placed in the original tomb. Since then the concourse of visitors increases day by day. From all sides come requests for images and souvenirs of the sweet friend of the Blessed Virgin. She is invoked with a confidence that has often been rewarded by genuine grace of recovery, of conversion, of success in difficult matters. Numerous incidents have been carefully collected, after the most serious investigations, to help in the pursuance of her cause.

IV

THE SOUBIROUS FAMILY

We have frequently spoken of the surprising disinterestedness of the Soubirous, even in the most serious

THIS PHOTOGRAPH OF BLESSED BERNADETTE IN HER SHRINE WAS TAKEN
IN THE SPRING OF 1925, — FORTY-SIX YEARS AFTER HER DEATH

SHRINE CONTAINING THE BODY OF BLESSED BERNADETTE, IN THE
CONVENT CHAPEL OF NEVERS, FRANCE

and most trying circumstances,—regardless of the source whence came the offers of help. Such heroism merited them universal respect and admiration and contributed in a large measure to strengthen the word of Bernadette. But after the visionary's departure for the convent, the work of Lourdes being safely established, and supernatural intervention thoroughly proved,—this inflexible self-imposed rigor had lost its motive and everybody would have liked to see it disappear. This family's extreme poverty weighed upon the people of Lourdes in the shape of a remorse. It increased after Mrs. Soubirous' death,—for both father and children were thrown into a sort of stupor.

The venerable Abbé Peyramale,—and others thought as he did, attributed this staunch resistance to secret orders given to Bernadette on the part of the Celestial Lady and he most urgently prayed Mary to revoke them. He figured having found in a chance circumstance, Heaven's answer to his supplication. One day he learned that the Lacadé Mill, once occupied by the Soubirous and birthplace of Bernadette, was for sale. This bit of news came to him as a ray of light. Without delay, accompanied by Abbé Sempé, Superior of the Missionaries of the Grotto, he left for Tarbes in order to consult his Bishop relative to a project he had conceived. It was a question of buying the mill and turning it over to Mr. Soubirous who, with his children, might derive some benefit therefrom. Not only did

Bishop Laurence approve this plan but he voluntarily offered to meet all expenses personally.

It was thus that François Soubirous, to the satisfaction of all, became proprietor of the Lacadé Mill. And so was Bernadette's family guaranteed a decent livelihood for the rest of their days.

V

THE CHALLENGE OF MR. E. ARTUS

In 1871, following the miraculous recovery of his niece, Juliette Fournier, through the medium of the water of Lourdes, Mr. E. Artus published a pamphlet in which, after he had related this wonderful favor, he launched in the face of the adversaries of the supernatural a bold challenge: it consisted of a wager of ten thousand francs which he proposed to pay to whosoever would prove before a jury composed of eminent men, to be taken from the different branches of the Institute, that any two miraculous cures related by Mr. Henri Lasserre, were frauds. This challenge was given a tremendous amount of publicity either by means of the press which reproduced it or by the diffusion of the pamphlet which could boast, after a few years, of more than fifty editions. Mr. Artus deposited the required amount with Mr. Turquet, notary public, No. 6, Hanover St., Paris, and to this sum was added five thousand francs. He waited patiently for many years hoping that some opponent would come forward and cover the amount. The freethinker, so proud and so audacious when he can do nothing but deny and blaspheme, is not quite the same man when he is called upon to make good his denials. Mr. Artus had found the proper means of compelling him to admit, at least tacitly, his bad faith, his cowardice, and his helplessness.

This challenge had placed the freethinkers in such an awkward position before the wide-awake public that one of their number, a man of prominence, attempted to take up the gauntlet,—but without meeting the proposed stake. This was Dr. Diday of Lyons, a man of great reputation as practitioner but especially as collaborator of medical reviews. He published therefore a very learned thesis, but punctuated it with so much hatred that one could classify it as a pamphlet. Bernadette, he qualified as one afflicted with hallucination,— the so-called miracles, as natural cures. Mr. Artus, in a clever reply, had no trouble in proving to him that of all the arguments, the most effective would be to accept the challenge in the proposed conditions, and that to refuse would be equivalent to a defeat. And such was the way the public understood, as also without doubt, the imprudent doctor himself who in time dropped the matter entirely.

But the adventure had its results. Dr. Diday, compelled by his interventions to study at close range the doings at Lourdes, was not long in discovering the truth and in admitting the existence of the supernatural. He was of good faith and he proved that he was logical.

From a militant freethinker he became a practical Catholic, casting away human respect when it was a question of reciting his rosary. He died with the sacraments of the Church in 1902, invoking the Immaculate Virgin whom he had ridiculed. The Blessed Virgin has oftentimes sought vengeance in this particular way against her adversaries. Following are a few more examples:—The Protestant doctor, Piou de St. Gilles, became a Redemptorist under the name of Reverend Father de St. Gilles; Dr. Longo, former anarchist, entered the order of the Recollets; Dr. Bull, an American-born Protestant, a noted atheist and freemason, was cured at Lourdes of all his infirmities of both body and soul. Without discontinuing the practice of his profession he applied himself with apostolic zeal to the conversion of heretics and many Protestants and even Jews are responsible to him for their conversion to Catholicism.

And these examples could be multiplied.

VI

THE CURES AT LOURDES

It is impossible to ascertain all the cures obtained at Lourdes and elsewhere by the use of the water of the Grotto. The majority escape the official investigations of the Ascertaining Bureau. Dr. Boissarie estimates at one-tenth of the total cures those that are entered in the official records, and he adds: "In compiling these facts we could truthfully say that from one thousand to fifteen hundred cures are effected annually at Lourdes." The records show that up to 1909, there had been three thousand eight hundred cures, many of them having been effected on the Court of the Rosary during the procession of the Blessed Sacrament. In the space of three years (1905-1908), these Eucharistic cures officially recorded, numbered one hundred and forty-eight.

An extraordinary spectacle characterized the National Pilgrimage of the Jubilee Year (August 21, 22, 23, 1908). A contingent of three hundred and fifty people, who had been cured miraculously, took part in the solemn procession with banners in hand. At their head could be noticed their dean, Justin Bouhohorts, the infant brought back to life on the day of the twelfth apparition, February 28, 1858.

VII

SHOULD LOURDES BE CLOSED IN THE NAME OF HYGIENE?

One of the French journalists, Jean de Bonnefon, most disqualified on account of his perfidy and his bad faith, his falsehoods and his calumnies against religion and the Catholic Church, assumed,—or rather was given the deplorable mission of overthrowing the work of Lourdes. It is easy to conjecture whence the order came. Lourdes, we all know, constitutes with Montmartre the great stumbling block of freemasonry. The object of the sect was to frighten and excite the public by making it understand that this constant influx of pilgrims, accompanied by the sick, might become a serious menace to public health.

This was placing the medical associations in a false light and a great number of its most authorized members despatched answers that he least expected.   On the appeal of Doctor Vincent, professor and former surgeon of Charity Hospital at Lyons, three thousand physicians protested by open letter.   Amongst these physicians favorable to Lourdes, we find 13 members of the Academy of Medicine, 52 professors of Faculties or Schools of Medicine, 129 Hospital Physicians or Surgeons, 65 former Heads of the Departments of Clinic and Laboratory; 203 former interns of the Hospitals of Paris, Lyons, and the Provinces.   And thus failed most miserably, through the medium of the scientists themselves, this hypocritical assault engineered in the name of science.

A journal writer, Mr. Bauster, has published a book in which he gives a list of 346 physicians, including 16 university professors, who all have testified in writing that there are cures performed at Lourdes which are a mystery to science and which defy all rational explanation through the mere forces of nature.

VIII

THE PHYSICIANS AT LOURDES

The clinic at Lourdes is one of the most astonishing creations of our times.   Founded in 1887 by Doctor de St. Maclou, who died in 1892, (Dr. G. Boissarie succeeded him and remained as president until he died in 1917) at a time when man repudiates the idea of the supernatural, when the mere mention of the word *miracle* produces sneers of unbelief, it required audacity to establish a public enterprise whose sole object is the study of the miracle. And this institution is open to all the scientists of the world,—especially to physicians, regardless of their nationality, of their philosophical or religious doctrines. And this call has been wonderfully answered, due no doubt to the mighty influence which mystery exercises upon the human soul. To speak of physicians only, over three thousand six hundred, whose names are contained in the registers or written underneath a record which attests the presence of a miracle, have frequented this strange institution. They hail from every country. Many of them are Protestants, Jews or freethinkers.[1] All are given the same welcome, all are perfectly free to study the many cases submitted.

How many there are who were sceptical at the outset but who emerged from this clinic convinced! How many are found who, having for years denied the existence of a miracle, left there their prejudices of education and schools! How many conversions, miraculous fruit of miraculous cures, owe their origin to Lourdes!

[1] In 1908, during the period of the great pilgrimages, the Bureau was visited by 625 physicians. One of these, a Protestant and professor at Fordham University, New York, Dr. E. Jeliffe, wrote as he returned from his visit: "Everything proceeds at Lourdes with the most perfect loyalty, the methods in vogue dispel even the faintest conception of fraud."

The clinic of Lourdes extends its action to the hospital of Our Lady of Seven Dolors, where the sick pilgrims of the poor class are lodged,—and to the Ascertaining Bureau established on the circle of the Court of the Rosary. It is there that those who have been cured miraculously are led in order to undergo an examination by the physicians present.

IX
OUR LADY OF LOURDES AND JOAN OF ARC

We outline briefly from "La Semaine Religieuse d'Arras" (January 14, 1910) an interesting narrative taken at Arras from the lips of Bishop Schoepfer of Tarbes, who witnessed the incident personally. It was the third day of the National Pilgrimage of 1909; all had prayed with exceptional fervor, and still no miracles whatsoever; even at the procession in the afternoon no cures had been registered. The Blessed Sacrament had been returned to the tabernacle and the people were beginning to disperse, when suddenly a powerful voice intoned the hymn in honor of Joan of Arc: "Sonnez, fanfares triomphales . . ." The strains were taken up by the entire gathering. The first verse was barely finished when cries were heard along the entire line of the sick; they were acclamations in honor of Our Lady of Lourdes and Joan of Arc followed immediately by the "Magnificat" sung by twenty-five thousand voices. The words "cures," "miracles," fly through the crowds

ROOM WHERE BERNADETTE DIED

HOME OF BERNADETTE

CHAPEL AT NEVERS
Which contains the remains of Bernadette

who press on towards the Ascertaining Bureau. What happened? During the singing in honor of Joan of Arc a number of cures were effected in quick succession, and the pilgrims thus favored, protected with difficulty from the surging masses by the stretcher-bearers, had run to the Bureau to undergo a thorough examination by the physicians. These cures numbered thirteen or fourteen. . . .

All these miraculous recoveries constituted for the blessed Liberatrix of France a new and brilliant glorification prepared by our Lord and His Immaculate Mother.

X

THE BANNERS OF ALSACE AND OF LORRAINE

The marvelous victory which in November, 1918, brought to a close the greatest war in the history of the world, had for its primary effect the return to France of two provinces which were taken from her in 1871. Ever since that sinister epoch, their banners, draped in mourning,—(emblems of regret and hope) were suspended as a continuous prayer from the ceiling of the basilica of Lourdes. This prayer was heard and rewarded; the exiled provinces once liberated, these mourning draperies became out of place. It was therefore expedient that they disappear. The Bishop of Tarbes and Lourdes, Mgr. Schoepfer, an Alsacian by birth, conceived the happy idea of surrounding this function with great solemnity. The eleventh of February, 1919, the anniversary of the apparitions at Massabielle, was selected for this patriotic manifestation. Amidst a vast concourse of pilgrims comprising twelve Bishops and a numerous clergy, a procession was formed at the Church of the Rosary leading to the Grotto; it was headed by a military contingent composed of English, Portuguese, American, Belgian, and French soldiers, representing all the allied nations whose coöperation had brought the deliverance of the captive provinces. Before the blessed Grotto, his Lordship Archbishop Richard of Auch removed the insignia of half a century's mourning from the two noble banners which, having been transformed into symbols of victory, resumed their places among all the other French banners in the temple of the Immaculate Virgin, Queen of Victory.

At the same moment an identical ceremony took place at Paris in the Church of Our Lady of Victories under the presidency of His Eminence Cardinal Amette.

Glory be to God! Thankfulness and gratitude to Mary!

A. M. D. G.